100

THINGS TO DO IN
TUCSON
BEFORE YOU
DIE

2nd Edition

D0840581

100

THINGS TO DO IN

TUCSON
BEFORE YOU
DIE

2nd Edition

CLARK NORTON

DEDICATION

To Conrad and Felix, the first native Tucsonans in our family, and
to their parents, Grael and Nona, who convinced us
to make Tucson our home.

CONTENTS

Sports and Recreation

• •

Culture and History

● ●

Shopping and Fashion

ACKNOWLEDGMENTS

I would like to thank the following people for their valuable assistance on the second edition of *100 Things to Do in Tucson Before You Die*: Dan Gibson, Cynthia Meier, Brad and Maria Lawrence, Roland Sarlot, Susan Eyed, Tom Skinner, Amy Soneira, Justin Germain, Jennifer Allen, Linda Wolfe, Mitch Stevens, Tom Philabaum, Kathleen Hayes, Margaret Feinman, Emily Borchers, Jessi Kyte, Howard and Diana Kohn, Michael and Mary Reiter, Veronica Daly, Sheldon Clark, Tom and Chris Sonnemann, Michael Livermore, Lia Norton, and Mary Beth Norton. Special thanks go to Josh Stevens and all the folks at Reedy Press for giving me the opportunity to write this book; to Grael Norton and Nona Patrick, who first introduced me to Tucson and continue to advise me on all their favorite things to do here; and to my wife, Catharine Norton, who has accompanied me throughout my research, made indispensable suggestions on the manuscript, and truly made this book possible.

—Clark Norton, Tucson, Arizona

PREFACE

In this new second edition of *100 Things to Do in Tucson Before You Die*, you'll find a number of recurring themes: life in the desert, the history of the Old West, the influences of Spain and nearby Mexico (which at one time both claimed this region), the pulsating culinary and arts scenes, the rebirth of downtown Tucson, and the the many contributions of the University of Arizona to the intellectual and cultural life of the city. Also covered in these pages is the remarkable range of recreational opportunities here: hiking, biking, horseback riding, golfing, ballooning—and rooting for the Arizona Wildcats and other local teams.

Compared to much of the United States, Tucson's climate turns the calendar on its head: winter, not summer, is when most events take place. The "season" for outdoor and even many indoor activities runs roughly from September or October until April or May, before the searing summer heat (up to 115 degrees Fahrenheit!) sends most everyone scurrying indoors or to cooler climes. Some attractions shorten their hours or close down altogether from June to August. Those Tucsonans who brave summer in the Old Pueblo, as the city is known, enjoy uncrowded roads, plenty of seating at their favorite restaurants (at least the ones that remain open), the welcome respite of drenching monsoon rains, and bragging rights to being true desert denizens—even if they have their central AC to thank.

• •

Tucson's 550,000 residents (and a million in the metropolitan area) have much to be proud of. In 2015 Tucson was named the country's first "UNESCO City of Gastronomy" in recognition of its longtime native culinary heritage, sustainable agriculture, and thriving food scene. Its downtown—once nearly deserted at night and on weekends—is now buzzing with new hotels and residential apartments, cutting-edge restaurants and bars, sold-out concerts, and festivals of every description.

But Tucson has always been known for its independence of thought and action, its love and respect for the desert environment, its frontier heritage, and its cultural diversity. The city somehow manages to absorb seemingly contradictory elements—rodeo riders and Rhodes scholars, stately saguaros bordering busy boulevards, the young and hip mingling with graying retirees—and meld them all into a vibrant whole. (The retirees, it must be noted, can be pretty hip themselves.)

As I've discovered, there are far more than 100 things to do in Tucson, but in the book you'll find an intriguing mix of well-known attractions and off-the-beaten-path gems that even many residents may not be aware of—or have never gotten around to trying. To that end, *100 Things to Do in Tucson Before You Die* is intended to appeal to residents as well as visitors—including the many hybrid "snowbirds" who flock down from the frozen north to spend their winters here in sunshine and 70-degree weather.

Whether it's a secluded hiking trail in the nearby mountains or the frenetic action of a 100-mile bike race, a place to sip local craft beers or sample the messy delights of a Sonoran hot dog, a visit to a museum of miniatures or the country's largest gem show, a ticket to the county fair or the symphony orchestra, you'll

• •

find the whys, the wheres, and the hows within these pages—and much more. So welcome to a Tucson that may surprise you—and will almost certainly charm you—as you explore the Old Pueblo, whether for a weekend or a lifetime.

Special notes: As was true for the rest of the country and the world, the pandemic forced long-term shutdowns of many attractions and amenities in Tucson. Some that were featured in the first edition of this book did not survive. But most (and several brand-new ones) have weathered through, while still facing the possibility of occasional bumpy rides ahead. While every effort was made to include the latest information on all 100 activities in this book, it's always a good idea to double-check for any updates or disruptions first by calling or going online.

FOOD AND DRINK

TREAT YOURSELF
TO TOP-FLIGHT TACOS AT BOCA

One of the most celebrated chefs in Tucson specializes in making tacos. But not just any tacos. Maria Mazon has ridden her exceptional cooking skills to recognition by the James Beard Foundation and a high finish on TV's *Top Chef* competition. And she's taken her restaurant, BOCA Tacos y Tequila, along for the culinary joyride. Born in Tucson and reared in Sonora, Mexico, Mazon draws inspiration from both and produces highly original, authentic, cooked-to-order tacos at her casual eatery (with roomy patio) along busy North 4th Avenue.

Choose among a tempting variety of meat, vegetarian, and seafood tacos, such as the puerco verde (shredded pork in tomatillo sauce); the cauliflower (grilled with curry cilantro and orange oil); and the camaron (chipotle-marinated shrimp). Accompaniments include a flight of (still warm) house-made tortilla chips with several different—and delicious—salsas.

533 N 4th Ave., 520-777-8134
bocatacos.com

TIP
Each Wednesday, Mazon features a special
Latin-flavored *El Menu de la Chef*, "until we run out."

TASTE THE TOWN
WITH TUCSON FOOD TOURS

In a decade of leading Tucson Food Tours, Bradner Lawrence has seen his company catch fire (but never fear, he's a firefighter by trade). He began by leading four-hour lunchtime strolls through downtown, where—along with stops at five or six eateries—the gregarious Lawrence spun entertaining tales of local history, architecture, and culinary lore. Now Tucson Food Tours has expanded to offer similar food-oriented rambles along North 4th Avenue and Main Gate Square (just off the UA campus). And for beer lovers, a new afternoon "brewstilleries" tour has joined the repertoire.

The food tours allow ample time to sample an array of tasty tidbits. Stops range from well-known city restaurants to hidden pearls. While the tours mainly attract out-of-towners, some Tucson residents also sign up, eager to discover more about their own city.

520-477-7986
foodtourstucson.com

TIP
Each tour is limited to 12 participants.
Reserve your tour at least 48 hours in advance.

GATHER IN THE COURTYARD
AT THE MERCADO

Located at the western end of the Sun Link streetcar line in a rapidly developing area on the edge of downtown Tucson, the Mercado San Agustin has established itself as a thriving Mexican-style public marketplace since opening in 2010.

While shops are part of the draw, the food offerings are an even bigger enticement. You can choose among upscale New American dining at Agustín Kitchen (520-398-5382, agustinkitchen.com) or casual but exceptional Mexican fare at Seis Kitchen (520-622-2002, seiskitchen.com); pick up some baked goods at La Estrella Bakery (520-393-3320) or Dolce Pastello Cakes (520-207-6765); sip a coffee or Mexican hot chocolate at Presta Coffee Roasters (520-333-7146); cool off with a raspado at Sonoran Sno-Cones (520-344-8470); or pick up fresh produce at a weekly Thursday farmers' market.

The pleasant setting includes table seating in a spacious, open-air inner courtyard, built in the Spanish Colonial style.

100 S Avenida del Convento, 520-461-1107
mercadodistrict.com

TIP

At the MSA Annex down the street from the Mercado (267 S Avenida del Convento)—a complex of shipping containers transformed into mini-shops—you'll also find outdoor eateries such as Beaut Burger and Kukai Fresh Japanese Kitchen.

TAP INTO THE CRAFT BREWING CRAZE
AT BORDERLANDS

Tucson's craft beer scene is hopping, with new breweries opening every year. Dozens of brewery-based taprooms now welcome beer lovers eager to sample the latest handcrafted creations.

Borderlands Brewing Co., which opened in 2011 in a historic 1890s-era warehouse downtown, has helped set the pace. Priding itself on its Southwestern style, Borderlands turns to regionally grown ingredients, such as cactus fruit juice in its Prickly Pear Wheat Ale, to provide its brews with a local personality. An "Arizona Beer Tour" menu—which can be sampled in flights of four and varies seasonally—is a popular feature and may include brews such as a Dillinger IPA and a Baja Girl Blonde.

Borderlands is also a lively and fun place for tastings—especially in its outdoor beer garden, which comes complete with a bocce court, live music several nights a week, and other events.

119 E Toole Ave., 520-955-9826
borderlandsbrewing.com

TIP
During the annual mid-February Tucson Craft Beer Crawl you can sample beers from more than 30 brewers at a dozen venues in downtown Tucson.
tucsoncraftbeercrawl.com

Here are other top craft breweries to try,
including one of the signature beers for each:

1912 Brewing Co. (Peppercorn Saison)
2045 N Forbes Blvd., 520-256-4851
1912brewing.com

Barrio Brewing Co. (Tucson Blonde Ale)
800 E 16th St., 520-791-2739
barriobrewing.com

Dragoon Brewing Co. (Dragoon IPA)
1859 W Grant Rd., 520-329-3606
dragoonbrewing.com

Firetruck Brewing Co. (Salida del Sol Amber)
4746 E Grant Rd., 520-777-9456
firetruckbrewing.com

Iron John's Brewing Co. (Old Pueblo Pale Ale)
555 E 18th St., 520-232-2080
ironjohnsbrewing.com

Ten55 Brewing Co. (XOXO Coffee Stout)
110 E Congress St., 520-777-7877
1055brewing.com

EAT AND GREET
AT TUCSON MEET YOURSELF

In 2015, when Tucson became the first American city to be honored as an UNESCO City of Gastronomy, the annual Tucson Meet Yourself festival helped illustrate why. This longtime folklife and food-filled event, held over a three-day weekend downtown each fall, is rooted in the concept that Tucson's gastronomy is intertwined with its history, culture, and surroundings.

Along with music, dance, and handicraft and cooking demonstrations, dozens of food trucks serving up ethnic specialties attract throngs of festival-goers. From Persian lamb and Peruvian *lomo saltado* to Jamaican jerk chicken and Filipino noodles, authentic foods from around the globe have added immeasurable depth and flavor to the city's gastronomic stew. Tucson Meet Yourself is more than just a food fest: it's a folk cultural experience—and a very tasty one indeed.

tucsonmeetyourself.org

TACKLE
A SONORAN HOT DOG

The Sonoran hot dog—one of Tucson's iconic foods—is no run-of-the-mill ballpark frank. Here's the recipe: start with a hot dog, wrap it in bacon, and grill. Place into a bolillo, a special roll that comes with closed ends so all the toppings don't drip out.

Toppings typically include beans, fresh onions, grilled onions, tomatoes, mayo, mustard, and hot salsa (fresh roasted chiles are optional, as are other items such as cilantro, radishes, and guacamole). Pick it up (or grab a fork if necessary) and consume.

While you can find Sonoran hot dogs at food trucks and pop-up stands around town, Tucson has two consistently popular purveyors: El Güero Canelo and BK Tacos.

El Güero Canelo (elguerocanelo.com), recent winner of a James Beard Foundation Award for America's Classics, has three locations; the one on South 12th Avenue offers the most local color. BK Tacos (bktacos.com) has two locations.

5201 S 12th Ave., 520-295-9005
2480 N Oracle Rd., 520-882-8977
5802 E 22nd St., 520-790-6000

BK Tacos
2680 N 1st Ave., 520-207-2245
5118 S 12th Ave., 520-295-0105

bktacos.com

SAVOR A PIE AND A PINT
AT REILLY

An Italian restaurant called Reilly? Well, yes, but that's not all that's unusual about this triple-threat establishment. Reilly Craft Pizza + Drink took its Irish-sounding name from the previous occupant, which happened to be a funeral parlor.

The main restaurant—which sports brick walls, wooden floors and a spacious, handsome bar area of its own—serves up top-flight small plates, pizzas, and pastas. The garage where the morticians kept the hearse now harbors 40 taps for the craft beer offerings, many of which are served in its comfortable indoor-outdoor beer garden upstairs. (A rooftop restaurant extension is also in the works.) And a single white arrow off the beer garden points downstairs to the speakeasy-style Tough Luck Club, where cocktails are the specialty. For an Italian restaurant named Reilly, it all makes perfect sense.

101 E Pennington St., 520-882-5550
reillypizza.com

TIP
Be sure to try Reilly's top-selling item: fried Brussels sprouts flavored with wine vinegar, hot sauce, and crumbled pecan brittle—addictive.

BINGE ON CHIMICHANGAS
AT EL CHARRO

El Charro Café—the oldest continually operated, family-owned Mexican restaurant in the country, dating from 1922—is also Tucson's best-known restaurant. Often filled to capacity with overflow crowds waiting outside, El Charro is housed in a historic Presidio District building that harbors an array of rooms and courtyards. Once seated, you can sip a margarita while trying to decide among the almost dizzying selection of Sonoran Mexican standards.

The huge *carne seca* platter—beef dried in the sun on the restaurant's roof, then shredded and grilled with chile, tomato, and onion and served with guacamole, rice, and beans—is a signature dish. Another is chimichangas, deep-fried guilty pleasures said to have been invented by El Charro's founder years ago when she accidentally dropped a burrito into frying oil and made Mexican culinary history.

311 N Court Ave., 520-622-1922
elcharrocafe.com

TIP
Two much newer El Charro branches are located north of downtown at 6910 E Sunrise Dr. (520-514-1922) and 7725 N Oracle Rd. in Oro Valley (520-229-1922). And if you missed dining at one during a visit, there's now a branch at the B gates of the Tucson International Airport.

STEAK YOUR CLAIM TO TRADITION
AT DAISY MAE'S

It wouldn't be cattle country without beef—or steakhouses. Some old-timers have been around since tumbleweeds drifted down Broadway Boulevard, while others are greenhorns. Daisy Mae's Steakhouse, open since 1990, falls between them in age but is a prime exemplar of this Tucson tradition.

There's nothing highbrow about the place; the most striking elements of the decor are the thousands of dollar bills with scribbled messages that have been tacked to the walls—most by patrons praising the food. Except for an extensive beer list, the menu is relatively short, focusing on beefy Angus steaks—rib eyes, T-bones, sirloins, and porterhouses expertly mesquite-grilled over an open flame—as well as tender baby-back ribs and chicken with delectably delicious skin (with some of the best wings in town). Baked potato, ranch beans, and Texas toast are squeezed onto the platter wherever they'll fit.

2735 W Anklam Rd., 520-792-8888
daisymaessteakhouse.com

Charro Steak—the newest entry in the steakhouse wars—char-grills its steaks over mesquite, Sonoran-style.
188 E Broadway Blvd., 520-485-1922
charrosteak.com

El Corral is a venerable house of beef that rides its cowboy theme all the way and carves its signature prime rib into four sizes.
2201 E River Rd., 520-299-6092
elcorraltucson.com

Silver Saddle, another old timer, is known for tender, flavorful rib eyes. Check out the antique mesquite bar in back.
310 E Benson Hwy., 520-622-6253
thesilversaddlesteakhouse.com

Mesquite-grilled steaks star at the **Horseshoe Grill**, which also smokes ribs, brisket, and salmon.
7713 E Broadway Blvd., 520-838-0404
thehorseshoetucson.com

FIND A FOOD TRUCK FAST

Tucson sports dozens of food trucks, serving up everything from pizza, hot dogs, burgers, and barbecue to Cajun, Vietnamese, Peruvian, and Mexican dishes. Much of it is of high quality, and some successful brick-and-mortar restaurants even operate their own trucks.

Trucks being trucks, though, they have a tendency to move around–a lot– in search of the next prime location or big event. But you don't have to go aimlessly cruising city streets to find the food truck of your dreams. The following sites enable you to search for food trucks by type of cuisine, by current or future locations, or by upcoming events where they are scheduled to appear.

Tucson Food Trucks
tucsonfoodtrucks.com

Roaming Hunger
roaminghunger.com/food-trucks/az/tucson

Tucson Food Truck Roundup
facebook.com/tucsonfoodtruckroundup

GET YOUR ASIAN FOOD FIX
AT LEE LEE SUPERMARKET

When Meng Truong immigrated to Arizona from Cambodia 30 years ago, he found himself making frequent trips to California to stock up on Asian foods that his wife missed from home. Eventually he decided to open his own markets in Arizona, situating one of his three Lee Lee International Supermarkets in Tucson. Initially catering to the growing Asian community, he soon expanded into other ethnic foods as well; the huge supermarket now carries products from more than 30 countries or regions around the globe. But the Asian foods still stand out.

The produce aisles alone, featuring an array of fruits and vegetables, many of them exotic to the desert, would be worth the trip. But there's much more, including one of the best selections of hard-to-find fresh and frozen seafood in Tucson, as well as long rows of spices and sauces and many specialty items.

1990 W Orange Grove Rd., 520-638-8328
leeleesupermarket.com

TIP

Adjacent to Lee Lee is Banhdicted, which specializes in banh mi (Vietnamese sandwiches). Try the lemongrass beef or the veggie. 1980 W Orange Grove Rd., 520-389-8128, banhdicted.com

SEEK OUT THE "HIDDEN" CHARMS
OF CAFÉ A LA C'ART

Some of Tucson's top attractions harbor small restaurants and cafés that serve top-flight food but are easily overlooked by tourists and residents alike. Café a la C'Art, situated within the Tucson Museum of Art, is a prime example. Even though it's not visible from the street, the café is accessible without paying museum admission.

It's an ambitious operation, serving breakfast, weekend brunch, lunch, and dinner. Both indoor and outdoor seating are attractive options. The indoor portion is located in a historic adobe that doubles as an art gallery, while the outdoor portion occupies an inviting covered patio with a trellis in the museum's courtyard. The lunch menu, in particular, sparkles with an array of inventive sandwiches, salads, and house-made pastries, a specialty. Chilaquiles, salmon cakes benedict, and a variety of omelets star at breakfast and brunch.

150 N Main Ave., 520-628-8533
cafealacarttucson.com

Here are some other often-overlooked eateries located within various attractions around town:

Edna's Eatery, within the Tucson Botanical Gardens (admission required), puts a Southwestern spin on breakfast and lunch. 2150 N Alvernon Way, 520-326-9686 x 37 tucsonbotanical.org/cafe

LaCo Restaurant (formerly La Cocina), offering eclectic Latin-style dishes, occupies a secluded courtyard within the Old Town Artisans shopping complex. 201 N Court Ave., 520-622-0351 lacotucson.com

The Garden Bistro at Tohono Chul serves "breakfast with butterflies," lunch, and Sunday brunch. 7366 N Paseo del Norte, 520-742-6455 tohonochulpark.org

HAVE A FEAST AT ...
FEAST

If you name your restaurant "Feast," you'd better deliver the goods—and owner-chef Doug Levy does just that, turning out a cascade of inventive dishes. Levy doesn't just offer duck; he'll make "seared Long Island duck breast, served over pickled peach sticky rice with nasturtiums, Russian honey-cake croutons, and a peach nectar-brown butter sauce." And it's not just menu verbiage—the flavors stand out, and everything seems to gel.

Feast changes its menus the first Tuesday of each month, to keep things seasonal and fresh. The menu is the same for lunch and dinner, so if you're a Feastling, as Levy dubs his regulars, you can try out a number of dishes. It does mean, though, that the dish you loved in April will be gone in May. Feast is also known for its wine bar and high-class wine shop.

3719 E Speedway, 520-326-9363
eatatfeast.com

TIP

Chances are that, at some point, a man dressed like a chef will greet you at your table—that's Doug Levy, and he may well stop to chat about your opinion of the meal.

MEET AT MAYNARDS
FOR A MEMORABLE MEAL

Located within Tucson's 1900s-era Historic Train Depot, Maynards Market and Kitchen offers a close-up view of the many trains that rumble through the city. Chances are, though, you'll be paying such rapt attention to your food—some of the city's finest and freshest cuisine—that the train whistles will pass without notice.

The Kitchen is open for dinner nightly and brunch on Sundays, serving classics such as cassoulet, pan-roasted duck, and bouillabaisse—using locally sourced ingredients, including greens from its own garden. At Sunday brunch, you can sit inside or out on the patio near the tracks, savoring the baked eggs, one of the city's best brunch dishes.

The self-service Market, open for three meals a day with both indoor and patio seating, serves up inventive sandwiches—the Cubano and grilled veggie stand out—as well as tasty soups, salads, and bowls of mussels.

400 N Toole Ave., 520-545-0577
maynardstucson.com

TIP
The restaurant is also known as the gathering point for Monday evening "Meet Me at Maynards"—free, loosely organized two-to-four-mile walks and runs through downtown; maps indicate restaurants along the routes (including Maynards) that offer discounts to registered participants.

REFRESH YOURSELF
WITH *RASPADOS*

They're one part sno-cone, one part shaved ice, one part fruit- or nut-topped ice cream sundae—often with *lechera* (sweetened condensed milk) poured over or Mexican candies sprinkled on top—and they come with fresh-fruit flavors such as mango, strawberry, pineapple, banana, cherry, lemon-lime, and blueberry.

In short, *raspados* may not be quite like anything you've ever had the pleasure of tasting before, and on a hot day in Tucson, they are definitely a pleasure. The safest bets for finding great raspados are on the south side of the city.

TIP
An iconic Tucson institution, eegee's, offers its own version of frozen fruit-flavored drinks. With 27 locations throughout the city, you're never far from one.

The city has numerous places
to sample *raspados*, including:

Marymar Raspados
4764 S 6th Ave., 520-746-1977

Michoacán Taqueria Raspados
3235 N Flowing Wells Rd., 520-888-0421

Oasis Fruit Cones
4126 S 12th Ave., 520-741-7106

Raspados El Paraiso
5917 E 22nd St., 520-398-5817
7701 Golf Links Rd., 520-886-2889

Raspados La Niña
5835 S Park Ave., 520-273-8611

Sonoran Sno-Cones
120 S Avenida Del Convento,
in the Mercado, 520-344-8470

FEEL THE VIBE
AT SAINT CHARLES TAVERN

Tucson has its share of old-favorite bars, but new waves of watering holes are making a splash by creating ever-more inventive cocktails, uncorking regional wines, and dispensing local craft beers from the tap. Saint Charles Tavern manages to bridge the gap between the two. Though open only since 2016, it has such a casual neighborhood vibe that it seems like it's been around for years.

That neighborhood is South Tucson, a small city within the larger city—not far from downtown, replete with Mexican restaurants, but not yet gentrified. (It may, however, become Tucson's next hip hotspot.) Saint Charles's welcoming service, eclectic vintage-industrial decor, and extensive selection of cocktails and craft beers—along with the pool tables, the juke box, and the outdoor area with a music stage where local bands appear, make for a winning combination.

1632 S 4th Ave., 520-888-5925

TIP
Saint Charles doesn't serve food, but you can
bring your own or even have some delivered there.

Here are some other bars that have
come on the scene in the past few years:

At **HighWire**, you can sample the results of
"molecular mixology."
14 S Arizona Ave., 520-449-8673
highwiretucson.com

Owls Club is an atmospheric gathering spot with a
speakeasy vibe in a stylishly renovated mortuary.
236 S Scott Ave., 520-207-5678
owlsclubwest.com

Playground has an inviting rooftop terrace
overlooking the action downtown.
278 E Congress St., 520-396-3691
playgroundtucson.com

R Bar, next to the Rialto Theatre, packs in the
before- and after-show crowds, indoor and out.
350 E Congress St. on Herbert Alley, 520-305-3599

Sky Bar is a solar-powered café by day,
an astronomy bar by night.
536 N 4th Ave., 520-622-4300
skybartucson.com

Tap & Bottle pulls in the crowds
with 20 craft beers on tap.
403 N 6th Ave., 520-344-8999
7254 N Oracle Rd., 520-268-8725
thetapandbottle.com

JUMPSTART YOUR MORNING
AT 5 POINTS RESTAURANT

Located a few blocks south of downtown at an intersection where five streets meet, 5 Points Market and Restaurant quickly became a neighborhood fixture after opening in 2014. Serving breakfast, lunch, and brunch, it fills up fast with a crowd of regulars who often greet one another, conduct casual business meetings amid the brick-walled industrial decor, snag a table on the small outdoor patio, or just settle in to sample some of the best morning fare in Tucson.

Relying on locally sourced ingredients, 5 Points' dishes are made from scratch, juices freshly squeezed, and espresso drinks properly strong. Among other savory items, they turn out some of the best huevos rancheros in town, combining local eggs with sharp white cheddar, house-made ranchero sauce, cilantro-serrano pesto, and fresh tortillas. Sandwiches and salads are popular fare at lunch. The adjoining 5 Points Market carries organic produce and dairy.

756 S Stone Ave., 520-623-3888
5pointstucson.com

MAKE BRUSHFIRE BBQ
A TO-GO GO-TO

Tacos, burritos, burgers, and pizza may be the top choices for to-go food in Tucson, but the BrushFire BBQ Co. deserves a spot in the rotation. The slow-smoked brisket and pork are so tender and scrumptious that the BrushFire food truck gives away generous samples of each at various street fairs around town, luring many passersby to order a sandwich even if they had other lunch or dinner plans.

At BrushFire's two restaurant locations, they serve up a full menu of smoked meats and more that also includes ribs (pork or beef), chicken, turkey, salmon, pork belly, and wings. They're all given a dry rub and then gently smoked for hours before being dabbed with the sauce of your choice. Several tasty sides are also available—as are family-sized portions.

2745 N Campbell Ave., 520-624-3223
7080 E 22nd St., 520-867-6050

brushfirebbq.com

DINE LIKE A TUCSONAN
AT TITO & PEP

Since it opened in late 2018, word about Tito & Pep, which bills itself as "Midtown's Neighborhood Bistro," quickly spread well beyond its neighborhood, earning plaudits from local food critics and customers alike. The chef-owner, John Martinez, describes his fare as "not Mexican, it's 'Tucsonan,'" which translates to expertly prepared dishes such as steak skewers with chipotle-tomatillo salsa and mesquite-grilled salmon with mayacoba beans. Desserts—the dark chocolate ganache is a favorite—are memorable, and the setting is attractive but casual enough to be comfortable.

Creative cocktails with local flavor (the Padre Kino, the Sam Hughes, the Catalina Sunrise, and the Conquistador's Mule) show the mixologists know their way around the Old Pueblo. But where did the name Tito & Pep originate? Those were imaginary characters Martinez's grandmother invented as a girl to entertain her younger sister. Fortunately, the restaurant named after them is for real.

4122 E Speedway Blvd., 520-207-0116
titoandpep.com

SAMPLE MEXICO'S DIVERSE CUISINE
AT PENCA

Of the "Best 23 Miles of Mexican Food" that Tucson claims, it's safe to say that at least 20 of those miles represent the dishes that most Americans—and Tucsonans—know best and adore: tacos, burritos, enchiladas, and the like, identified with the province of Sonora due south of the city. But, good as they are, they don't begin to encompass the breadth of Mexican cuisine.

Penca Restaurante, which specializes in the food of central Mexico, survived a wave of downtown restaurant closings during the pandemic. Located in a century-old building that exudes an air of rustic chic, Penca now offers revamped seasonal menus that draw on both their classic dishes and the bounty of the Sonoran desert. Watch for items like *nopales* (grilled prickly pear cactus) and *lubina* (branzino marinated in coconut mole blanco). And yes, Penca also serves authentic—and delicious—tacos.

50 E Broadway Blvd., 520-203-7681
pencarestaurante.com

TIP
Penca has opened a very pleasant patio out front,
sporting the ambiance of a European café.

MUSIC
AND ENTERTAINMENT

HEIGH HO,
COME TO THE FAIR

Tucson's largest family-oriented event, the Pima County Fair, has been packing in the crowds since 1911. An annual, week-long blowout, it lights up the Pima County Fairgrounds in late April, generally just as the weather is getting warm—but still cool enough not to melt the kids' ice cream cones before they can get them under control.

Carnival rides and games, concerts large and small—including the likes of Tanya Tucker and the Village People at previous fairs—percussive dance performances, petting zoos, kiddie areas, tractor pulls, rodeos, antique car shows, horse shows, pony rides, sea lion encounters, wildlife exhibits, animal barns, livestock auctions, demolition derbies, and beer fests are all typically on tap.

And, of course, you can chow down on a mountain of guilty-pleasure food that you might never eat except at the Pima County Fair.

11300 S Houghton Rd., 520-762-3247
pimacountyfair.com

TIP
At other times of the year, the Pima County Fairgrounds hosts Tucson Speedway races (tucsonspeedway.com) and Southwestern International Dragway races (tucsondragway.com). Check their websites for schedules.

PUNCH YOUR TICKET TO BROADWAY
IN TUCSON

A staple of top-quality entertainment since 2004, Broadway in Tucson performances grace the stage at the 2,500-seat Centennial Hall on the University of Arizona campus. Each season, which extends from September to the following April, attracts a half dozen or so nationally touring productions of hit Broadway shows past and present, sometimes featuring stars direct from the originals.

Broadway in Tucson productions have included *Hamilton, My Fair Lady, The Lion King, Mamma Mia, Cabaret, Phantom of the Opera, Rent, West Side Story, Fiddler on the Roof, The Sound of Music, Avenue Q, Motown: The Musical,* and *The Book of Mormon*—selling out many engagements and drawing audiences totaling upwards of a half million people. Centennial Hall dates from 1937 but has generally good sight lines to the stage and underwent major acoustics upgrades in 2007.

1020 E University Blvd., 800-745-3000 (tickets)
broadwayintucson.com

TIP
The restroom facilities at Centennial Hall are in dire need of an upgrade—cramped, with long lines the norm—so you may want to limit your liquid consumption.

SET YOUR CALENDAR
FOR 2ND SATURDAYS

The concept is simple: Line up some bands to provide live music on multiple stages downtown; invite food trucks to serve concessions; coordinate with nearby restaurants, attractions, and businesses; and give it a name everyone will remember. That name—"2nd Saturdays"—even marks your calendar for you, since these free outdoor street festivals take place the second Saturday of every month.

The music varies—you may find a punk rock band on one stage and a Pink Floyd cover band or an all-female surf rock band on another—and the evening hours vary somewhat by season (earlier in winter, later in summer). But the formula remains the same: offer quality, family-friendly music and food, and they will come—every 2nd Saturday.

E Congress St. and S Scott Ave., 520-268-9030
2ndsaturdays.com

TIP
You can ride the Sun Link streetcar downtown from the North 4th Avenue-UA campus area, look for free street parking after 5 p.m., or park in one of three inexpensive downtown garages (Pennington Street, Depot Plaza, or Centro).

MAKE YOUR WAY
TO THE MONTEREY COURT CAFÉ

It's easy to pass the Monterey Court Café and never realize that one of Tucson's most enjoyable and prolific music venues lies hidden within. A neon sign still reads "Monterey Court," a motel built in 1938 that sat at the eastern end of the Miracle Mile, once one of the city's prime lodging strips. In 2011 the motel closed and was transformed into an artisan enclave complete with music stage, galleries, shops, and a café serving upscale food and drink. Over the past decade, Monterey Court has hosted more than 2,000 concerts.

The dining patio offers good views of the courtyard stage, where live music fills the air every evening from Tuesday through Sunday, as well as a Sunday brunch. Open-air or covered seating can accommodate nearly 300 people. Musical genres vary nightly—you may encounter jazz, blues, Western swing, African soul, rockabilly, or anything else.

505 W Miracle Mile, 520-207-2429
montereycourtaz.com

TIP
It's always a good idea to call for reservations here.

TUNE IN
TO THE TUCSON SYMPHONY

Back in 1929, when the Tucson Symphony Orchestra tuned up its first violins, it was a group composed of mostly amateur musicians playing in a school auditorium. Today, as a highly accomplished professional orchestra whose main venue is the nearly 3,000-seat Music Hall at the Tucson Convention Center, it performs a number of "Classic" and "MasterWorks" concerts each season (September to April) along with a variety of ensemble performances and chamber orchestra, pops, and children's concerts. Award-winning, globe-trotting musical director José Luis Gomez brings incredible energy to the stage.

The TSO has also added a Youth Orchestra and Symphony Chorus, and it periodically appears in smaller venues around Tucson: a high school, a church, its own Symphony Center, and even at top local restaurants for its "Moveable Musical Feasts." Each holiday season, the Symphony Chorus performs Handel's *Messiah* accompanied by the symphony's Chamber Orchestra.

Tucson Music Hall: 260 S Church Ave.
Box Office: 2175 N 6th Ave., 520-882-8585
tucsonsymphony.org

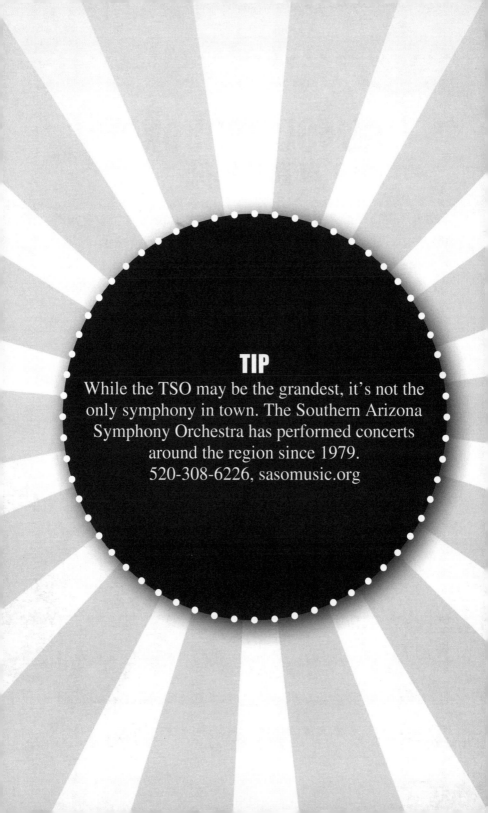

TIP

While the TSO may be the grandest, it's not the only symphony in town. The Southern Arizona Symphony Orchestra has performed concerts around the region since 1979.
520-308-6226, sasomusic.org

GO FOR PROVOKE
AT THE ROGUE

Performing in an intimate theater converted from a former gym, the Rogue Theatre presents a lively and eclectic assortment of five plays each season from September to May. For nearly two decades, the talented ensembles have served up award-winning, often-innovative productions by modern-day and classical dramatists, such as *Death of a Salesman, Mrs. Dalloway,* and *Twelfth Night.* (One Shakespeare play is on the docket every year.)

Why "Rogue"? The Latin origin of "rogue"—*rogare*—means "to ask," and the company regards its mission as presenting plays that offer challenging and provocative points of view. Creative Director Cynthia Meier writes and directs some of the top productions herself, including a recent adaptation of Herman Melville's *Moby Dick* that was both ambitious in its scope and powerful in its impact. Tackling a 2,000-page classic for the stage? That's going Rogue—and it works.

300 E University Blvd., 520-344-8715
Box office: 520-551-2053
theroguetheatre.org

TIP

Tickets are general admission except those reserved for season ticket holders. But in this cozy, comfortable theatre, all 160 seats offer excellent viewing.

HAVE A GUFFAW
AT THE GASLIGHT

Don't go to the Gaslight Theatre expecting serious drama, but you can expect some seriously funny melodrama, set to the often boisterous backdrop of a tinny piano, corny jokes, and audience laughter. Staging five original shows per year—often musical spoofs of popular movies (*Space Wars, Back to the Past*)—Gaslight has developed a devoted clientele while honing its shtick since 1977. Feel free to cheer the good guys and boo the villains; audience participation is encouraged.

Table seating permits you to munch and sip suds or soda along with the action on stage. While the performers are more polished than the food—pizza, nachos, and such—it's fine for a casual, family-friendly meal (and the popcorn is free). Each production runs six nights a week for two to three months; Mondays are concert nights, often covering country, rock, or pop music artists.

7010 E Broadway Blvd., 520-886-9428
thegaslighttheatre.com

TIP
A recent offshoot, the Gaslight Music Hall,
showcases an array of tribute bands.
13005 N Oracle Rd., Oro Valley, 520-529-1000
gaslightmusichall.com

CATCH A FLICK
AT THE LOFT CINEMA

Tucson has plenty of cookie-cutter multiplexes airing many of the same blockbuster movies, but if you're yearning for something different, head to the Loft Cinema. Since 1972, the Loft has been treating Tucsonans to the best—and often the most offbeat— movies ever made. Whether it's current or classic cinema, foreign or domestic, Hollywood or indie, musicals or documentaries, commercial or art films, the Loft has it all—and shows many of them on the largest screen in southern Arizona. Expert commentaries accompany some special screenings.

Among their ongoing series are Cult Classics (*Harold and Maude, Blade Runner*) and Mondo Mondays (horror films). On some Friday nights, they invite would-be *auteurs* to submit their own short films for showings, but if you're among them, be forewarned: if the audience doesn't like it, you'll get gonged.

3233 E Speedway Blvd., 520-795-0844
loftcinema.org

TIP
Tucson hosts the 11-day Arizona International Film Festival in late April each year, the oldest and largest film fest in the state (520-401-4328, filmfestivalarizona.com). And each March, Tucson Cine Mexico adds to its standing as the longest-running festival of contemporary Mexican cinema in the country (tucsoncinemexico.org).

Other places to find distinctive
film-going experiences include:

The **RoadHouse Cinema**, where you can
recline your seat, put your feet up, and order food
and drink to be brought to you during the show.
4811 E Grant Rd., 520-468-7980
roadhousecinemas.com

Cinema La Placita, which shows $3 classic
movies outdoors in the plaza at the Tucson
Museum of Art every Thursday at 7:30 p.m. from
May to August, and even throws in the popcorn.
140 N Main St., 520-326-5282
cinemalaplacita.com

At the **Cactus Carpool Cinema**, which found a
permanent space in 2021 after 10 years of
sporadic existence, you can enjoy old-fashioned
drive-in movies with food-truck concessions.
6201 S Wilmot Rd., 520-372-2124
cactusdrivein.com

The Screening Room shows classic and indie
films and hosts the Arizona International
Film Festival.
127 E Congress St., 520-882-0204
screeningroomdowntown.com

WATCH TOP PERFORMERS
AT ARIZONA ARTS LIVE

The University of Arizona offers a treasure trove of music and other entertainment on campus, including performances by world-renowned artists as well as by talented students and faculty members.

The headlining shows are brought in under the umbrella of Arizona Arts Live (formerly UA Presents), which attracts top-name entertainers—singers, dancers, musicians, and more—to perform in varying venues, mostly on campus. Shows have run the gamut of star power, from the Warsaw Philharmonic Orchestra and violinist Izhak Perlman to singer Chaka Khan and the Peking Acrobats. Campus venues include 2,500-seat Centennial Hall, 600-seat Crowder Hall, and the 295-seat Stevie Eller Dance Theatre. But with its name change to Arizona Arts Live, UA is reaching out to serve off-campus venues as well, from the 1,164-seat Fox Tucson Theatre downtown to smaller stages across the region.

520-621-3341
arizonaartslive.com

Lesser-known campus productions
range from drama to music and dance:

"See Tomorrow's Stars Today" at **the Arizona
Repertory Theatre**, as UA theater majors
perform in six main productions each season,
one of which is always a Shakespeare play.
Marroney and Tornabene Theatres
1025 N Olive Rd., 520-621-1162
theatre.arizona.edu

The Fred Fox School of Music presents
concerts and recitals by UA faculty and
students as well as by guest artists.
1017 N Olive Rd., 520-621-1655
music.arizona.edu

The UA Dance Ensemble features
professionally trained student dancers
performing ballet, modern, and jazz dance.
Stevie Eller Dance Theatre
1713 E University Blvd., 520-621-1162
tickets.arizona.edu

GUSSY UP
FOR THE OPERA

Prepare to be swept away by the majesty of vibrant baritones, soaring sopranos, and vivid costuming and sets. In its five decades, Arizona Opera has produced more than 170 fully staged operas and concerts, and now presents five grand operas each fall-to-spring season at the Tucson Music Hall in the Convention Center.

Recent productions have included *Madame Butterfly*, *Rigoletto*, *Carmen*, *La Bohème*, *La Traviata*, and *The Marriage of Figaro*, as well as operettas and operas by Arizona composers. Arizona Opera has also staged Wagner's demanding four-opera *Ring Cycle* twice—a feat accomplished by just a handful of other American opera companies. Musicians drawn from three Arizona symphony orchestras as well as a chorus of talented local vocalists add depth to the productions.

260 S Church Ave. (Tucson Music Hall)
Box office: 520-293-4336
azopera.org

TIP

Never fear if you aren't fluent in the many languages of opera. English translations are displayed on a screen above the stage as the performers vocalize, and the printed programs contain synopses of the often complex and scandalous plots.

BE MYSTIFIED
AT CARNIVAL OF ILLUSION

It's an evening of "Old World Magic" with healthy doses of mystery, danger, and "ooh la la" tossed in. And Carnival of Illusion—a two-person show performed by the engaging couple Roland Sarlot and Susan Eyed—delivers plenty of laughs and vaudeville-style showmanship to boot.

Playing off a Victorian-era world travel theme, Sarlot and Eyed smoothly deliver a slew of "how did they do that?" magical moments—pulling off sleight-of-hand, card, and memory tricks; swallowing razor blades; defying gravity; cutting a woman in half; and making US currency miraculously appear inside freshly cut fruit. Each year they have some new tricks up their sleeves, and there's plenty of audience participation along the way as well. Everyone leaves smiling—and suitably mystified.

Like good magicians, you never know where they might appear: it could be at the ornate Scottish Rite Cathedral downtown, or just out of a hat in less formal venues—so check their website or call for the latest information.

480-359-7469
carnivalofillusion.com

SWAY TO THE MUSIC
AT THE DESERT SONG FESTIVAL

In much of the United States, summertime is music festival season. Not so in sunbaked Tucson, where musicians gather in cooler months to celebrate life with instrument and song. Since 2013, the Tucson Desert Song Festival has blossomed into a citywide musical extravaganza that extends for three weeks from January into February and has attracted talent of international stature in multiple genres.

Performers have included Broadway's Kristin Chenoweth, guitarists Rene Izquierdo and Adam del Monte, and pianists Michael Barrett and Steven Blier. Vocalists from classical to pop—Bobby McFerrin was a recent performer—chamber orchestras, jazz and Latin musicians, ballet troupes, medieval ensembles, and tributes to artists such as Leonard Bernstein appear in city venues large and small, from the spacious Tucson Music Hall and Fox Tucson Theatre to the more intimate Leo Rich Theater and UA's Crowder Hall.

888-546-3305
tucsondesertsongfestival.org

You can also check out these other popular seasonal music festivals:

Tucson Jazz Festival: Jazz junkies gather at venues around the city each January for ten days of concerts that span most every genre.
520-762-6260
tucsonjazzfestival.org

Gem and Jam Fest: Coinciding with Tucson's huge Gem and Mineral Show each February, this three-to-four-day fest features everything from acid rock to reggae, bluegrass fusion to funk, and Afrobeat to disco.
gemandjamfestival.com

Tucson Folk Festival: One of the largest free (and family-friendly) folk music festivals in the country attracts musicians from throughout the Southwest for two days of music and dance in early April, at several different venues.
tucsonfolkfest.org

DIVE INTO DANCE
AT THE BALLET

Ballet Tucson brings high-quality dance to the desert, producing a mix of classical and contemporary ballets each season (November to May). Founded in 1986, the ballet had developed into a fully professional dance troupe by 2004, and now its roster has two dozen artists who have danced professionally with companies throughout the United States, including the American Ballet Theatre, the New York City Ballet, and the Dance Theatre of Harlem.

As part of its cultural mission and extensive community outreach programs, the ballet company also nurtures a children's ensemble that performs alongside the pros in productions such as *Cinderella*, *Sleeping Beauty*, and its annual holiday presentation of *The Nutcracker*. Performances take place in major venues around the city, including the Temple of Music and Art and the Tucson Music Hall downtown, and the Stevie Eller Dance Theatre on the UA campus.

520-903-1445
ballettucson.org

TIP

Watch for the possible return of "pop-up performances," live dance works held outdoors at various venues around the city, which proved to be hits when the 2020 regular season was cancelled during the pandemic.

TAKE IN A PLAY
AT THE ATC

Splitting its time between Tucson and Phoenix, the Arizona Theatre Company (ATC) has produced well over 200 plays, including several world premieres, in its more than half-century history. Performing on the main stage in Tucson's historic Temple of Music and Art, the ATC's professional cast and staff have staged works ranging from classic Shakespeare and Molière to contemporary playwrights like Sam Shepard and Athol Fugard. Musicals and lighter fare are also on the docket. Almost all the costumes, sets, and props are produced in-house.

With its front courtyard, fountain, and Mexican tile, the Spanish Colonial Revival–style Temple of Music and Art makes an attractive venue. Besides the main 623-seat Alice Holsclaw Theatre, the Temple also houses the 80-seat Cabaret Theatre and an art gallery. The annual theater season runs from September to April.

330 S Scott Ave., 520-622-2823
arizonatheatre.org

CRUISE TO A CONCERT
ON CONGRESS

Two legendary Congress Street grand-dame theaters with similar storied histories—the Fox and the Rialto—have been key to the revival of downtown Tucson as a thriving entertainment hub.

The Art Deco Fox Tucson Theatre, once dubbed downtown's "Crown Jewel," dates from 1930, when it was a movie and vaudeville venue. After the mid-1970s, it was closed for 30 years before being extensively restored in 2006. The 1,164-seat theater now presents nationally known musical acts, theatrical productions, and film screenings.

The 1,200-seat Rialto Theatre debuted in the 1920s hosting silent movies and vaudeville acts. After extensive renovations in the 1990s and 2000s, it now attracts about 200 musical acts annually—indie and rock bands, jazz musicians, country singers, and more—along with other entertainers. Within walking distance of the UA campus, the Rialto often draws a big student crowd.

Fox Tucson Theatre
17 W Congress St., 520-547-3040
foxtucson.com

Rialto Theatre
318 E Congress St., 520-740-1000
rialtotheatre.com

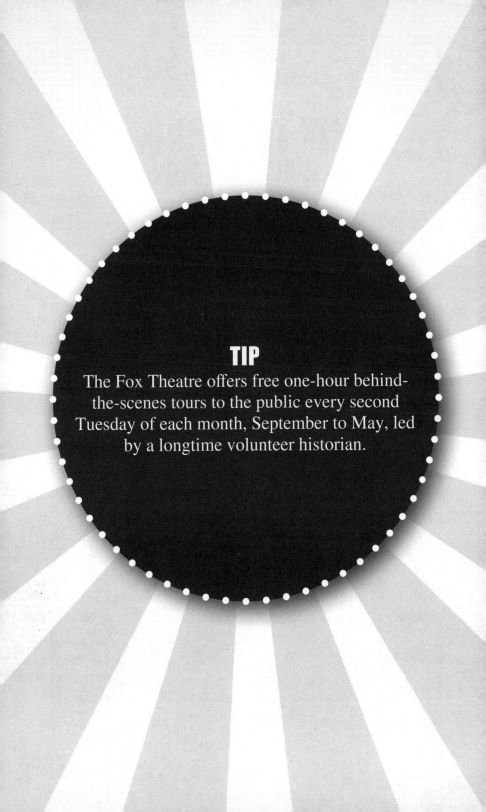

TIP

The Fox Theatre offers free one-hour behind-the-scenes tours to the public every second Tuesday of each month, September to May, led by a longtime volunteer historian.

HIT THE TRAIL
TO TRAIL DUST TOWN

If it weren't surrounded by the rest of Tucson, Trail Dust Town might eventually evolve into Trail Dust Metropolis. Opening in 1961 with a cowboy steakhouse and some shops bearing an Old West theme, Trail Dust Town has mushroomed over the decades into a family-friendly (and family-owned) entertainment complex that includes live Western stunt shows, amusement park rides (including a Ferris wheel and an antique carousel), a miniature train, a gold-panning area, a shooting gallery, a day spa, an 1890s-style saloon, and an old-time photography studio—as well as the "pioneer-era" shops and steakhouse that started it all. No need to don your fancy finery; the watchword here is "No ties allowed."

Trail Dust Town doesn't come fully alive until the evenings; hours vary by the activity and season, so check the website for each.

6541 E Tanque Verde Rd., 520-296-4551
traildusttown.com

TIP
You can pay by the individual activity or purchase
unlimited access to most attractions for an entire evening.

MOSEY ON OVER
TO THE MAVERICK

After the rodeo—or just when you have a hankerin' for two-stepping out on the town—Tucson's Maverick has been the place to go since 1962. The eastside "King of Clubs" offers line dancing lessons on "Wild West Wednesdays" and Saturdays, Arizona rhythm two-step lessons on Thursdays, country swing lessons on "Fireball Fridays," cowboy brunches on the weekends (with bottomless mimosas and country music on the patio), and Wednesday to Sunday happy hours from 3 to 7 p.m. DJs spin some tunes, but live country bands often appear later in the evenings.

Along with ample supplies of beer and margaritas, including daily specials, the Maverick has a dinner menu with standard fare like burgers, wings, nachos, and fish and chips. But the real action is on the dance floor—so don't forget to don your best Western finery.

6622 E Tanque Verde Rd., 520-298-0430
tucsonmaverick.com

COZY UP TO THE BANDS
AT 191 TOOLE

You shouldn't have trouble finding 191 Toole; its address is its name (though technically the address is 191 E. Toole). And once you get there, you'll find a lot to like. The sound system and acoustics are first rate, the staff is friendly, tickets and beer are reasonably priced, and the restrooms are clean. The maximum number of concertgoers is 500. And as a sister venue to the larger Rialto Theatre, 191 Toole attracts some top regional and local bands and some touring national bands as well.

You may find the more popular concerts to be standing room only, and when it fills up, it can get hot in the summer. But if you want to hear Tommy Castro and the Painkillers, Miss Olivia and the Interlopers, and the Heartless Bastards as they were meant to be heard, 191 Toole is the place.

191 E Toole Ave., 520-445-6425
191toole.com

TIP
Paper tickets are available at the Rialto box office during their office hours; the 191 Toole box office opens one hour before the show starts.

You might also like these other
small- to medium-sized music venues:

Club Congress, located in the historic Hotel
Congress, features live music some nights and
DJs spinning dance tunes on others. Watch for the
free Spring Concert Series on the outdoor plaza.
311 E Congress St., 520-622-8848
hotelcongress.com/club

The **Sea of Glass Center for the Arts** attracts
local, national, and international performers,
with an emphasis on world music.
330 E 7th St., 520-210-4448
theseaofglass.org

HEAR THE VOICES
OF THE BORDERLANDS

Borderlands Theater didn't choose its name lightly. Founded in 1986, this Tucson-based professional company has focused most of its productions on the people who live in the US-Mexico border region, with special emphasis on Latino and Native cultures. A recent production, *Antigone at the Border*, a contemporary reimagining of the Greek classic, put a creative spin on current border patrol controversies.

With the goal of creating greater understanding within the borderlands and giving voice to often-overlooked segments of the population, it has developed and produced dozens of plays by new and established playwrights on topics as weighty as immigration and as routine but intimate as daily life. But it has also staged lighthearted holiday season shows lampooning the year's most lampoon-able events. Borderlands productions appear in venues around the city.

151 S Granada Ave., 520-276-9598
borderlandstheater.org

GAMBLE AND GAMBOL
AT TUCSON'S CASINOS

Local Native American tribes own and operate two prominent casinos on tribal lands just outside Tucson, which serve up the requisite games of chance and more.

The Casino Del Sol, run by the Pascua Yaqui Tribe, has branched out beyond its 1,300 slot machines and blackjack and poker tables to stage outdoor concerts and other productions at the 4,400-seat AVA Amphitheater, Tucson's largest venue. The more intimate Tropico Lounge also offers nightly entertainment.

Over at the Desert Diamond Casinos & Entertainment, owned and operated by the Tohono O'odham Nation, they're promising Arizona's "biggest uncapped jackpots," with poker, blackjack, bingo, and keno all featuring high-stakes games. After testing your luck, celebrate or commiserate at the Monsoon Nightclub, which hosts a variety of national musical acts.

Casino Del Sol
5655 W Valencia Rd., 855-765-7829, casinodelsolresort.com

Desert Diamond Casinos & Entertainment
7350 S Nogales Hwy., one mile south of Valencia Road, 866-332-9467
ddcaz.co

TIP
A second Pascua Yaqui Tribal casino, to be located on
W. Grant Ave. near I-10, is in the planning stages.

SPORTS AND RECREATION

EXPLORE
A DESERT OASIS

For many Tucsonans, hiking and Sabino Canyon are virtually synonymous. With its palm trees, creeks, hillside cacti, picnic areas, and glimpses of local wildlife, the Sabino Canyon Recreation Area is a place to escape urban life just a short drive from the city. It lies in the Coronado National Forest in the foothills of the Santa Catalina Mountains and is crisscrossed with trails ranging from easy nature walks to steep, rugged treks.

Transportation to upper Sabino Canyon, where many of the trails lie, is restricted to hikers, cyclists, and Sabino Canyon Crawler shuttle riders. The narrated 3.7-mile, one-hour roundtrip shuttle makes nine stops and operates daily, every half hour in winter and otherwise hourly. Passengers can disembark at any stop to hike, then catch the Crawler back from any stop. A separate shuttle runs every half hour to a trailhead in Bear Canyon.

5700 N Sabino Canyon Rd., 520-792-2953 (shuttle)
sabinocanyoncrawler.com

TIP
Some of the trails are risky in high water, and the road to Upper Sabino Canyon may flood at points as well. Waterproof shoes come in handy winter to spring; carry plenty of drinking water every season.

ELEVATE YOUR DAY
ON MOUNT LEMMON

Tucsonans head here in summer to escape the heat and in winter to ski in the snow at the nation's southernmost slopes. Spring through fall, they seek out its hiking trails, picnic areas, and panoramic views. Birders add to their life lists here, stargazers scan the brilliant night skies, and rockhounds admire its striking geological formations.

Mount Lemmon, at 9,157 feet the highest peak in the Santa Catalina range, looms some 7,000 feet above Tucson's northern foothills and offers recreational opportunities at every elevation and season. Allow an hour or more to drive to the top via the twisting Catalina Highway; scenic lookouts, hiking trailheads, and campgrounds beckon along the way. Or, if you're biking it—well, good luck. At the end of the road, the community of Summerhaven offers a limited number of restaurants, shops, and accommodations.

visitmountlemmon.com

TIP

On a sunny winter day, you could conceivably hit Tucson's tennis courts in the morning and Mount Lemmon's ski slopes that afternoon; temperatures at the summit are often 30 degrees cooler than in the city.

HEAD UNDERGROUND
AT KARTCHNER CAVERNS

Had it not been for two young explorers who happened upon a tiny passageway leading underground back in 1974, we might never have known about their remarkable spot: the vast, pristine "live" cave system now known as Kartchner Caverns. Remarkably, the men kept their discovery secret for 14 more years, and it wasn't until 1999 that the site opened to the public as a state park, about 50 miles southeast of Tucson.

The caverns are known for their strange and colorful limestone formations, including long, icicle-thin stalactites and drapes that resemble bacon and noodles. Two separate half-mile-long tours guide you through. The one-and-a-half-hour Rotunda/Throne Tour includes the discoverers' original trail, while the one-and-three-quarter-hour Big Room Tour focuses on some of the most unusual formations. Tours using only light from headlamps are offered most Saturdays. You can also camp, hike, and picnic in the park.

2980 S AZ Hwy. 90 (nine miles south of Benson)
877-697-2757 (cave tour reservations); 520-586-4100 (park information)
azstateparks.com/kartchner

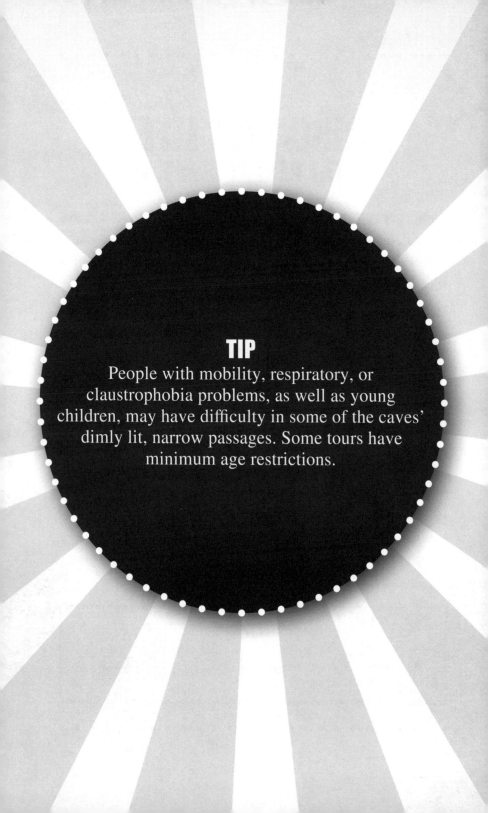

TIP
People with mobility, respiratory, or claustrophobia problems, as well as young children, may have difficulty in some of the caves' dimly lit, narrow passages. Some tours have minimum age restrictions.

DISCOVER LIFE
AT THE DESERT MUSEUM

Tucson is all about life in the desert, so it's appropriate that the Arizona-Sonora Desert Museum is the city's top visitor attraction. Forget any preconceptions about the desert being a stark place with little plant and animal life. And set aside any notions that this is a typical museum—the Desert Museum is primarily an outdoor experience, covering 21 acres and harboring some 1,200 types of plants and 300 animal species.

Besides enjoying exceptional views of mountains and valleys, you can follow trails to watch for wildcats, coyotes, and bighorn sheep; enter an aviary where native hummingbirds fly freely around you; stroll through a landscaped cactus garden; and head underground to encounter creatures that emerge only in the dark of night. You'll discover that the desert is a thriving, complex ecosystem . . . and anything but deserted.

2021 N Kinney Rd., 520-883-2702
desertmuseum.org

TIP
To best adapt to desert life yourself, wear a hat, sunscreen, and good walking shoes and take advantage of the shaded ramadas and drinking fountains scattered throughout the facility.

GO GLOBAL
AT THE INTERNATIONAL WILDLIFE MUSEUM

Though not far down the road from the better-known Arizona-Sonora Desert Museum, the International Wildlife Museum is (you might say) a completely different animal. The former has live desert animals, while at the latter, all the wildlife on display are permanent taxidermied residents from around the globe.

That said, the International Wildlife Museum's collection of over 400 preserved mammals, birds, and insects (all donated after their deaths) reside in well-designed exhibits and have the advantage of always being visible when you visit—plus you can view them up close without fear of a lion snacking on your arm.

Kids, especially, may be surprised to see just how big some animals (including a few prehistoric creatures) are at close range. The museum prides itself on supporting wildlife conservation efforts and educational outreach programs for children.

4800 W Gates Pass Rd., 520-629-0100
thewildlifemuseum.org

TIP
The museum shows movies like *Wild Detectives: Penguins* and *Animal Mysteries* throughout the day in its Wildlife Theater.

BROWSE THE BEAUTY
OF THE BOTANICAL GARDENS

The Tucson Botanical Gardens display an alluring array of desert plant life in the heart of the city. The five-and-a-half-acre gardens are divided into 17 specialty sections that illuminate a stunning variety of vegetation found in southern Arizona and in desert climes around the world.

They include crops and medicinal plants used by Native Americans, traditional Mexican-American neighborhood gardens, a children's discovery garden, a backyard bird garden, a miniature train garden, a Zen garden, a prehistoric garden, and (October through May) a delightful tropical butterfly and orchid pavilion. But the crown jewel is the cactus and succulents garden, showcasing dozens of species of cacti and related plants, both regional and from as far away as North Africa. An art gallery, gift shop, and indoor-outdoor café round out the attractions.

2150 N Alvernon Way, 520-326-9686
tucsonbotanical.org

TIP
Watch for special exhibitions from
October through May, as well as periodic guided tours.

STROLL
THE DESERT GARDENS
OF TOHONO CHUL

Along Tucson's northern fringes lie 45 acres of botanical gardens and desert landscapes honeycombed with walking paths and nature trails. At Tohono Chul, you can stroll through a desert palm oasis and a hummingbird garden, visit a "geology wall" built from rock specimens in the nearby mountains, and take your kids to a children's garden. Or tour an "ethnobotanical" garden displaying plants the local Tohono O'odham tribe employed to make medicines and baskets, then discover how to create a *sin agua* (without water) garden as well as a living desert courtyard at home.

Much of the emphasis is on learning how to nurture your own garden in the desert. Suitably inspired, you can purchase a wide range of cacti and other native plants from the greenhouse there, then browse the gift shop or have lunch at the Garden Bistro.

7366 N Paseo del Norte, 520-742-6455
tohonochul.org

TIP

Each year in mid-December, Tohono Chul stages its Holiday Nights spectacular, filling the gardens with more than a million twinkling lights accompanied by strolling musicians and food.

VISIT THE DARK SIDE
FOR STARRY, STARRY NIGHTS

The International Dark-Sky Association—dedicated to fighting the light pollution that obscures the stars in the night sky—was founded in Tucson. And while the city's growth means it's not quite the low-light city of years past, stargazing opportunities still abound under the region's night skies.

You might opt for periodic ranger- or naturalist-led night walks in Saguaro National Park East or West, or a "Cool Summer Nights" visit to the Arizona-Sonora Desert Museum for views of sunsets, stars, and nocturnal creatures from May to September. Or you could head up to the Mount Lemmon SkyCenter for stargazing high above the city, or out to the Kitt Peak National Observatory in the high desert 56 miles southwest of Tucson, where state-of-the-art telescopes await. Reservations are essential for all programs at both observatories.

Saguaro
National Park
520-733-5153 (East)
520-733-5158 (West)
nps.gov/sagu

Arizona-Sonora Desert Museum
2021 N Kinney Rd., 520-883-2702
desertmuseum.org

Mount Lemmon SkyCenter
520-626-8122
skycenter.arizona.edu

Kitt Peak National Observatory
520-318-8720 or 520-318-8739
visitkittpeak.org

HIKE
THE CATALINA CANYONS

Situated on one-time ranchland on the western edges of the Santa Catalina Mountains, Catalina State Park encompasses more than 5,000 acres leading up into craggy foothills and canyons. The park is thick with cacti—including thousands of majestic saguaros—and tall, slender ocotillos. In winter and spring, water courses through the canyons, feeding streams, pools, and waterfalls.

Short nature trails near the main trailhead provide a good introduction, but for serious hikers the rugged, often-steep five-and-a-half-mile roundtrip hike to Romero Pools via the Romero Canyon Trail ranks as one of the region's most beautiful treks, with sweeping views punctuated by saguaros, boulders, strikingly green desert vegetation (in season), and the refreshing sounds of rushing water. You might even spot bighorn sheep.

11570 N Oracle Rd., 520-628-5798
azstateparks.com

TIP
Other activities range from camping and picnicking to birding and horseback riding. Portions of the park are currently recovering from a devastating wildfire that swept through the Catalinas in 2020.

SOJOURN
WITH THE DESERT SENTINELS

Saguaros, the stately cacti that have served as the backdrop for countless Western movies, are found only in the Sonoran Desert, where Tucson resides. With their characteristic "arms," heights up to 50 feet, and lifespans up to 200 years, saguaros have been dubbed the sentinels of the desert—standing watch, in effect, over all other life-forms in this arid land.

To view them in their greatest natural splendor here, head to Saguaro National Park. Spread over more than 90,000 acres, Saguaro is actually two parks in one—West and East, separated by about 30 miles of cityscape and nestled in the foothills of two mountain ranges. Saguaro East is larger, but both offer multiple ways of exploring their saguaro forests: scenic roadways, hiking trails, nature walks, horseback rides, and picnic spots. The best months to visit—for cooler weather and more scheduled activities—are from October to April.

Saguaro East
3693 S Old Spanish Trail, 520-733-5153

Saguaro West
2700 N Kinney Rd., 520-733-5158

nps.gov/sagu

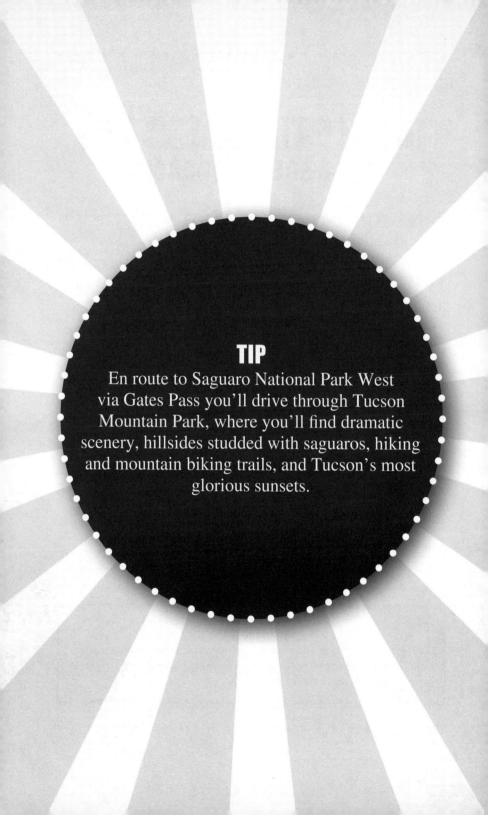

TIP

En route to Saguaro National Park West via Gates Pass you'll drive through Tucson Mountain Park, where you'll find dramatic scenery, hillsides studded with saguaros, hiking and mountain biking trails, and Tucson's most glorious sunsets.

TACKLE TUMAMOC HILL
FOR A SCENIC WORKOUT

Every week year-round, thousands of Tucsonans of all ages, body types, and fashion tastes set out to climb to the top of 3,100-foot-high Tumamoc Hill on the city's west side. A roadway leads 1 1/2 miles to the summit, 800 feet above the base, via a series of increasingly steep switchbacks.

The paved surface is well suited to the intrepid cardio hounds who run the route or push baby strollers. But most climbers take time to catch their breath and enjoy the hillside desert vegetation—cacti, ocotillos, palo verde trees—and watch for wildlife such as deer, rabbits, and reptiles (it's a University of Arizona ecological research center). Those who reach the top are rewarded with sweeping views of the city and surrounding mountains, and they can take comfort in knowing that the return is all downhill. Sunrise and sunset are prime climb times.

1675 W Anklam Road and Tumamoc Hill Road
520-621-6945 (Desert Laboratory)
tumamoc.arizona.edu

TIP
Download the Tumamoc Tour audio app (tumamoc.arizona.edu/outreach/tumamoc-app) to learn all about the hill's historical, cultural, and ecological importance as you navigate the hill.

FIND HANDS-ON FUN
AT THE CHILDREN'S MUSEUM

The best children's museums combine learning with fun, and the Children's Museum Tucson—whose focus is on creative play with a purpose—does exactly that. Since moving into the 1900-era former Carnegie Library building downtown in 1991, the action-packed museum has provided children of all ages (and their parents!) with roomfuls of imaginative, hands-on displays and activities.

Art and architecture projects, science experiments, climbing and exploring, playing with trains, and much more help kids and families discover a variety of fascinating new worlds. In Wee World, preschoolers can dress up in costumes or play musical flowers; in the Investigation Station, focusing on science, kids can check out the Bernoulli Blower or watch scarves fly through airways; and in Imagine It, they can play architect and engineer. Plan to stay a while, because most kids can't get enough of it.

200 S 6th Ave., 520-792-9985
childrensmuseumtucson.org

TIP

Children's Museum Tucson has a smaller branch in Oro Valley northwest of the city, which focuses on ages five and under. Young kids can try out the Lullaby Lounge, Peek-a-Boo Palace, and Toddler Town.
11015 N Oracle Rd., Oro Valley, 520-297-8004

CHEER FOR THE WILDCATS
ON THE FIELD AND COURT

On six or seven weekends from September through November, the University of Arizona plays home football games at 56,000-seat Arizona Stadium. A 112-foot-tall, 47-foot-wide video board—one of the largest and loudest in college football—helps spur the cheers. Block parties start on Fridays before the games, while game days bring tailgaters and the scents of grilling burgers to the UA Mall.

The toughest tickets in Tucson to land between October and March are for seats at UA men's basketball games, when the Wildcats regularly fill 14,545-seat McKale Center. A raucous student group dubbed the ZonaZoo leads a sea of red-clad fans in rocking the arena. And don't overlook the talented UA women's basketball team, which also plays at McKale Center. Both the football stadium and basketball arena are centrally located on the UA campus.

520-621-2287 (tickets)
arizonawildcats.com

TIP

In the spring, head to Hi Corbett Field in Reid Park to watch the UA men's baseball team or to Hillenbrand Memorial Stadium on campus to take in a UA women's softball game.

CYCLE
AROUND THE OLD PUEBLO

What will it be: a grueling 102-mile bike race or a five-mile fun ride? El Tour de Tucson, billed as "America's Largest Perimeter Bicycling Event," welcomes riders of all ages and abilities. For one day each November, cyclists wind through and around the city as they compete in races of 102, 57, and 28 miles. Kids can join Fun Rides of ten miles, five miles, or one mile. El Tour's long-distance races draw top competitors from around the world, while the fun rides draw thousands from around the block.

You'll have plenty of places to practice: the Tucson area offers 600 miles of striped bike paths, 300 miles of mountain biking trails, and 200 miles of residential bike routes. The Loop, a multi-use paved pathway that connects parks and trailheads around the city, totals more than 130 miles.

520-745-2033
eltourdetucson.org

TIP
Another test of speed and endurance, 24 Hours in the Old Pueblo, features teams of competing cyclists who pedal through the desert for 24 straight hours each February; the event attracts 2,000 riders annually (epicrides.com).

CHILL OUT
WITH ROADRUNNERS HOCKEY

Hockey in the desert played by a team called the Roadrunners, a bird known for speeding through arid terrain? If that seems odd, look at it this way: cooling off in an icy arena makes perfect sense in the Tucson heat. (Having a fan base supplemented by flocks of Canadian "snowbirds" who spend winters in the city doesn't hurt.)

The Roadrunners—the American Hockey League Pacific Division franchise that serves as the top minor league team for the National Hockey League's Phoenix-based Arizona Coyotes—relocated from Massachusetts to Tucson in 2016. The result has been a win-win for Arizona hockey: the wily Coyotes now have a nearby lode of talent to draw upon when needed, while Tucson gets to enjoy one of the world's fastest sports— fitting for a team of Roadrunners.

Tucson Convention Center Arena
260 S Church Ave., tickets: 866-774-6253
tucsonroadrunners.com

TIP
The Roadrunners' regular season runs from mid-October to mid-April.

ROOT FOR THE WOMEN
AT THE ROLLER DERBY

The flamboyant team names alone—Furious Truckstop Waitresses, Vice Squad, Bandoleras, Saddletramps—are enough to entice a newcomer to this action-packed sport. In 2003, local roller skaters helped found the Women's Flat Track Derby Association, and Tucson Roller Derby stars now compete against teams on city, state, and national levels throughout the year.

The action centers on "jammers" as they try to skate past opposing teams, evading blockers and trying to avoid penalties for grabbing, shoving, and tripping. Competitors are known for tattooed arms, a litany of injuries that only an orthopedist could love, and colorful monikers such as "Hollywood Killavard" and a librarian known as "Dewey Decimatrix." Bouts take place about once a month and typically attract raucous crowds to the Tucson Indoor Sports Center; check the website for dates.

1065 W Grant Rd., 520-624-1234 (Tucson Indoor Sports Center)
tucsonrollerderby.com

RIDE ON OVER
TO THE RODEO

Tucson's annual professional rodeo week, known officially as La Fiesta de los Vaqueros, is the time when local dudes and wanna-be cowgals dust off their 10-gallon hats, spit-polish their boots, don their spangled shirts, saddle up their minivans, and head to the rodeo grounds to cheer on the daring steer wrestlers, calf ropers, and barrel racers.

The late-February, eight-day celebration of cowboy culture—90 years and counting—is such a time-honored tradition that Tucson schoolchildren get part of the week off. (Local kids can also compete in their own rodeo events.)

During the week the Tucson Rodeo Parade features a procession of old-time horse-drawn carriages, buggies, and wagons along with cowboys on horseback, marching bands, and floats, all making their way through city streets to the rodeo grounds. It's said to be the world's longest non-motorized parade.

4823 S 6th Ave.
tucsonrodeo.com

Parade: 520-294-1280
tucsonrodeoparade.org

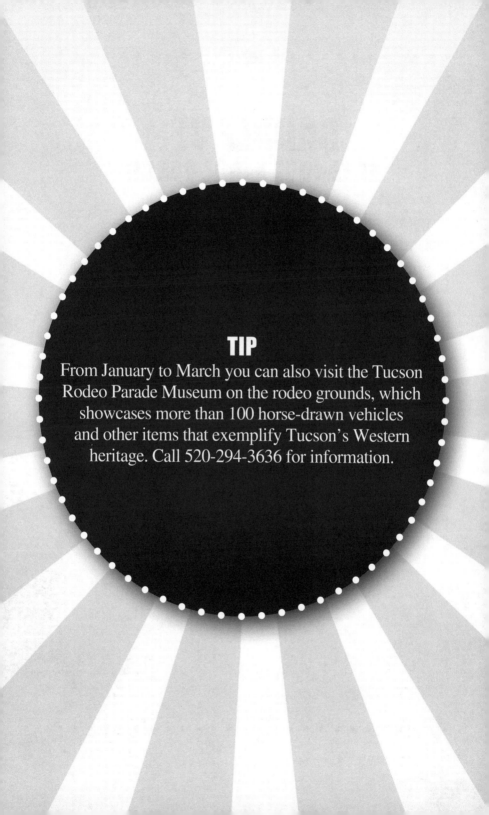

TIP

From January to March you can also visit the Tucson Rodeo Parade Museum on the rodeo grounds, which showcases more than 100 horse-drawn vehicles and other items that exemplify Tucson's Western heritage. Call 520-294-3636 for information.

SADDLE UP
AT TANQUE VERDE RANCH

If you've ever watched old Westerns, you've seen cowboys, Indians, and outlaws riding horses hell-bent across the saguaro-strewn Sonoran Desert hills near Tucson. At 650-acre Tanque Verde Ranch, often honored as one of the top family resorts in the country, you can saddle up and steer your mount over some of the same trails (the hell-bent part is optional).

While Tanque Verde's cattle-ranch roots go back 150 years and its dude-ranch roots date back for a century, today's version features luxury resort amenities like casitas with private patios, tennis courts, swimming pool, and spa. But those are mainly for shaking the dust off after a day exploring Saguaro National Park East and environs on horseback. The ranch, which keeps 150 horses and still runs a major cattle operation, offers a variety of trail rides, horsemanship lessons, guided hiking and biking trips, and kids' activities.

14301 E Speedway Blvd., 520-296-6275 or 800-234-3833
tanqueverderanch.com

The Tucson area offers a number of other guest ranches and stables where you can hit the trails on horseback. Here are some of the best:

Luxurious **Hacienda Del Sol Guest Ranch Resort** offers trail rides in the Catalina foothills. 5501 N Hacienda Del Sol Rd., 520-299-1501 or 800-207-6883; stables: 520-631-3787 haciendadelsol.com

Houston's Horseback Riding, run by a rodeo family, offers trail rides and lessons. 12801 E Speedway Blvd., 520-298-7450 tucsonhorsebackriding.com

Once a working cattle ranch, **Rincon Creek Ranch** is now a luxury guest ranch bordering Saguaro National Park East. 14545 E Rincon Creek Ranch Rd., 520-760-5557 rinconcreekranch.com

Saguaro Stables runs trail rides in Saguaro National Park East. 7151 S Camino Loma Alta, 520-298-8980 allaroundtrailhorses.com

White Stallion Ranch is a traditional dude ranch with desert rides. 9251 W Twin Peaks Rd., 520-297-0252 whitestallion.com

DRIFT OVER THE DESERT
IN A BALLOON

Drifting over the Tucson Mountains and Saguaro National Park West in a hot air balloon at sunrise is an unforgettable experience, and long-time balloon pilot Mike Fleury promises a safe, smooth, highly scenic ride for his four-to-five-passenger flights. Fleur de Tucson balloons ascend to heights ranging from 500 to 2,500 feet, permitting both close-up views of desert wildlife—perhaps javelinas, bobcats, foxes, and red-tailed hawks—and sweeping panoramas.

The 60- to 75-minute rides travel from 10 to 18 miles, varying with the wind currents. Safety comes first: balloons don't take off in strong winds, and Fleur de Tucson boasts an accident-free record. Fleury's wife, Becky, drives the "chase truck," which meets the balloon where it lands and carries champagne and breakfast fare to celebrating passengers. Ballooning season runs from October to April; allow three to three and a half hours in all.

520-403-8547
fleurdetucson.net

TIP
Families are welcome; weight limit per passenger is 275 pounds.

HIT THE GREENS
ON THE GOLF COURSE

Tucson's year-round sunshine and dry climate draw golfers from around the world. The region's 40-plus courses range from relaxing to championship caliber. (And no, they aren't just one big sand trap—there's plenty of greenery.) Choose among moderately priced but well-maintained municipal courses or more expensive and often-challenging resort courses, many of which are open to the public.

The top two 18-hole municipal courses are in Reid Park's Randolph Golf Complex: Randolph North—Tucson's oldest and longest public links—and the scenic Dell Urich (600 S Alvernon Way). Others are Silverbell (3600 N Silverbell Rd.), Fred Enke (8251 E Irvington Rd.), and El Rio (1400 W Speedway Blvd.).

Call 520-791-4653 to book tee times at any public course; check tucsoncitygolf.com for more information.

Top 18-hole resort courses are at the Lodge at Ventana Canyon (6200 N Club House Ln., 520-577-4092) and the Omni Tucson National Resort (2727 W Club Dr., 520-297-2271).

TIP
With the Mega Pass, cardholders can play unlimited rounds at all five city courses for eight months or one year, either weekdays or every day, including golf cart, advance reservations, and discounts on apparel and clubs. Prices start at $799.

ZIP OVER
TO THE REID PARK ZOO

Back in 1969, when it first opened its doors, the Reid Park Zoo was more like a glorified backyard menagerie than a real zoo. As the zookeepers describe it, they had only "birds, prairie dogs, farm animals, a few squirrel monkeys." But over the years the zoo, now fully accredited, has spread across 24 acres that harbor hundreds of animals and attract some 600,000 annual visitors.

Elephants, grizzlies, lions, tigers, rhinos, zebras, giraffes, lemurs, gibbons, macaques, ostriches, flamingos, tortoises, bearded dragons, skinks, macaws, and meerkats all make their homes here. There are also two aviaries: one with birds of the world and another with South American species. Giraffe Encounters, camel rides, the Zoo Train, and carousel rides—with 30 different species like anteaters and polar bears going round and round—are additional draws.

3400 E Zoo Ct., 520-791-3204
reidparkzoo.org

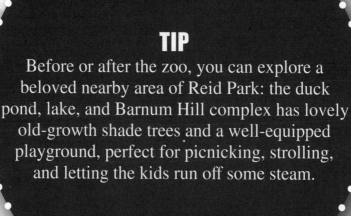

TIP

Before or after the zoo, you can explore a
beloved nearby area of Reid Park: the duck
pond, lake, and Barnum Hill complex has lovely
old-growth shade trees and a well-equipped
playground, perfect for picnicking, strolling,
and letting the kids run off some steam.

CULTURE AND HISTORY

VISIT EL PRESIDIO,
TUCSON'S BIRTHPLACE

Except for a small chapel situated at the foot of Sentinel Peak ("A" Mountain), the first European structure in Tucson was an adobe fort built in 1775 to protect a Spanish military garrison and settlers from Apache attacks. The northernmost point of the Spanish settlement of Arizona at that time, El Presidio San Augustín del Tucson featured four 750-foot-long walls up to four feet thick and 16 feet high, which stood for well over a century before the last section was razed in 1918.

Today much of the 11-acre site north of Congress Street houses government buildings, restaurants, museums, and shops, including some situated in historic 19th-century structures. The Presidio Museum, located on one corner of the original site, is a reconstruction of the fort and includes an authentic 2,000-year-old Native American pit house uncovered by archaeologists.

Presidio Museum
196 N Court Ave., 520-622-0594
tucsonpresidio.com

TIP
El Presidio is bounded by Washington,
Church, and Pennington streets and Main Avenue.

EXPLORE
THE OLDEST NEIGHBORHOOD

The name Barrio Viejo is Spanish for "old neighborhood"—fitting because this is where you'll find the oldest residential area in Tucson that remains largely intact. Most of the city's still-standing 19th-century Sonoran row houses are located here, many of them restored and serving as residences or offices.

Historic structures include the mid-18th-century Sonoran-style Coronet restaurant at the corner of West Cushing Street and South Meyer Avenue and the Teatro Carmen at 380 South Meyer (a one-time Spanish-language theater now being transformed into a 300-seat performance venue). The top landmark is El Tiradito—known as the Wishing Shrine—on South Main Avenue between Cushing and West Simpson Street. The same block has a small park that once harbored a natural spring and public baths.

visittucson.org

TIP
Situated just south of downtown, the barrio is roughly bounded by West Cushing Street on the north, South Scott Avenue on the east, West 18th Street on the south, and Interstate 10 on the west.

REVEL IN THE ROCKS
AT THE GEM AND MINERAL MUSEUM

Enjoying triple its previous space, the new University of Arizona Alfie Norville Gem and Mineral Museum adds serious heft and sparkle to downtown's museum scene. With one of the finest collections of its kind in the country—2,200 specimens—the museum's three galleries explore the evolution of minerals, the geology of Arizona and Mexico, and gem science, including interactive exhibits for all ages. Already on the map for its huge February gem shows, Tucson now further stakes its claim to global rock-star status.

Formerly housed in the cramped basement of the Flandrau Science Center and Planetarium on the UA campus, the collection now shines in the Historic Pima County Courthouse. Retired from judicial duties in 2015, the courthouse underwent a thorough restoration that has returned it to its original 1929 Spanish Colonial Revival–style glory, highlighted by a stunning blue-tiled mosaic dome.

115 N Church Ave., 520-621-7433
uamineralmuseum.com

TIP
The courthouse also houses the new Southern Arizona Heritage and Visitor Center (headquarters of Visit Tucson), as well as sites marking the 1934 Tucson arrest and arraignment of outlaw John Dillinger.

PEEK INTO
THE MINI TIME MACHINE

The Mini Time Machine Museum of Miniatures is the legacy of Tucsonan Patricia Arnell, whose lifetime of collecting superb miniature houses and room boxes began as a child with a single dollhouse. The 500-piece collection, which dates back to the mid-18th century, occupies more than 10,000 square feet of museum space and is attractively displayed in several uncrowded galleries.

The miniature houses and tableaux depict scenes fanciful and realistic, past and present, near and far. In keeping with the art of fine miniature-making, the detail work is often extraordinary, the scale of the tiny figures and objects—sometimes hundreds in one display—is precise, and elements of "wonder and whimsy" appear generously throughout. Exhibits range from evocative Christmas and Halloween scenes to antique houses, Edwardian inns, Irish fairy castles, and even dinner parties for dogs . . . all, of course, in miniature.

4455 E Camp Lowell Dr., 520-881-0606
theminitimemachine.org

TIP
Watch for special exhibitions, which sometimes
go behind the scenes to examine how artists create these miniature worlds.

TAKE A FLYER
AT THE AIR & SPACE MUSEUM

The Pima Air & Space Museum is so big that, much like some theme parks, it offers two-day tickets as well as one-day. Spanning a century of aviation history, it's one of the largest museums of its kind in the world, displaying more than 400 aircraft on 80 acres outdoors as well as five indoor hangars. Three of the hangars are devoted to World War II planes.

Allow at least three to four hours to cover the basics, but you could easily stay longer if you have the time and inclination—especially if you take additional tours of the adjacent Aircraft Boneyard, where the US government and military store planes. Boneyard tours are run from the Air & Space Museum but have separate ticketing procedures and restrictions; reservations are essential.

6000 E Valencia Rd., 520-574-0462
pimaair.org (Museum and Boneyard)

TIP
Guided walking tours are provided at several of the hangars, but tram tours are available for those who want or need to ride around the sizeable complex.

TOUR THE CHILLING
TITAN MISSILE MUSEUM

Once a top-secret underground military facility called Complex 571-7, the Titan Missile Museum housed nuclear-armed missiles in the Cold War era. Today it's a sobering reminder of the unthinkable threat of nuclear conflict.

Forty-five-minute guided tours visit the underground launch control center, where a 103-foot-high missile still sits in its launch duct, and take you through a tense simulated launch. The Titan II missile could deliver a nuclear warhead to a target more than 6,000 miles away within a half hour. To activate the missiles, the president would have sent coded messages to the officers at the site, who would then have gone through a "fail safe" process of authentication before launch—not knowing what the preprogrammed target would be. The site, located about 25 miles south of Tucson, was decommissioned in 1982 and is now a National Historic Landmark.

1580 W Duval Mine Rd., Green Valley (take exit 69 off I-19 S), 520-625-7736
titanmissilemuseum.org

TIP
Visitors taking the tour must be able to climb up and down 55 steps; there's no elevator access to the underground silo. However, the surface portion of the site is accessible to all.

GET LITERARY
AT THE FESTIVAL OF BOOKS

Mystery fans, cookbook aficionados, sci-fi nerds, poetry fanciers, and political junkies are among the book lovers who converge at the annual Tucson Festival of Books, which draws well over 100,000 people to the University of Arizona campus each March for a two-day celebration of authors and their work.

Since its 2009 debut, the event has blossomed into the third-largest book fest in the country, now attracting up to 400 authors, both big-name and under-the radar, who appear in panel discussions, cooking demonstrations, writer workshops, and book signings.

Much of the action takes place outside in big tents on the grassy Mall, where hundreds of exhibitors peddle books, performers entertain, food vendors dispense goodies, and authors gather to meet the public. Admission is free throughout, but many of the popular panel discussions require advance tickets.

tucsonfestivalofbooks.org

TIP

Bring the kids—the Science City tent and other displays geared toward youngsters from toddlers to teens are loaded with interactive activities, storytelling, and costumed characters.

ADMIRE THE ARTWORKS AND ADOBES
AT THE ART MUSEUM

The Tucson Museum of Art and Historic Block nicely melds the creations of top global and regional artists with a mix of contemporary and historic architecture. Drawing on its extensive permanent collections as well as temporary exhibitions, the museum's galleries—some situated within pioneer-era adobes—display paintings, drawings, indigenous crafts, and other artworks that range from pre-Columbian to postmodern. Special emphasis is devoted to the art of the American West, Native Americans, and Latin America.

Five 19th- and 20th-century structures stand within or are adjacent to the museum, part of the four-acre Historic Block where Tucson was born in 1775. These include the 1907 Mission Revival–style Corbett House, the mid-19th-century La Casa Cordova (Tucson's oldest adobe home), the 1868 (Edward) Fish House, and the mid-1860s Stevens/Duffield houses, which harbor the museum's excellent café.

140 N Main Ave., 520-624-2333
tucsonmuseumofart.org

HONOR THE DEPARTED
AT THE ALL SOULS PROCESSION

Inspired by the Día de los Muertos—the Mexican Day of the Dead celebration—the annual All Souls Procession has become one of Tucson's most iconic and revered public events. After modest beginnings in 1990, the procession, which is held in early November each year on or around All Souls' Day to honor and mourn the lives of deceased loved ones, now draws some 100,000 participants and spectators.

Mixing the colorful with the macabre, the procession includes giant skull art pieces, the Hungry Ghost busker troupe, costumed stilt-walkers, acrobats, drummers, and anyone who simply wants to join in. The two-mile route runs just west of downtown to the Mercado San Agustin, site of the dramatic finale, where a giant urn filled with wishes and messages for the departed is held high in the air and set ablaze.

allsoulsprocession.org

FOLLOW A DREAM
TO THE DeGrazia GALLERY

When Ted DeGrazia was unable to sell his artworks, he did what every unsung artist would like to do: he built his own galleries to display them. The Tucson artist, who died in 1982, is now well known; his desert landscapes and portraits of Native Americans have hung in major museums. But back in the 1930s and '40s, when he started work on his complex of Mexican-style adobes in the Catalina Mountain foothills, he labored in anonymity.

Building mostly by hand with the help of friends, he transformed 10 acres of cactus-strewn hillside into his own distinctive and at times eccentric studio in the sun. DeGrazia's voluminous body of work included hand-crafted jewelry and ceramics as well as paintings, but his Gallery in the Sun, which is now a National Historic District, may be his most enduring legacy.

6300 N Swan Rd., 520-299-9191
degrazia.org

TIP
A 2017 fire severely damaged the Mission in the Sun, the complex's chapel, and a number of original murals were lost. The chapel was restored and reopened two years later.

CELEBRATE PAST AND PRESENT
AT HOTEL CONGRESS

The Hotel Congress is Tucson's most famous lodging, anchoring a prime downtown location since 1919. Over the past century, the Congress has witnessed the city's transition from small town to bustling metropolis and has played a memorable role in Tucson's colorful history as well. Notorious criminal John Dillinger was captured in January 1934 after he and his gang, posing under aliases as normal hotel guests, were unmasked by local firemen.

Today, the Congress honors its history by preserving Dillinger-era touches in its rooms: rotary phones, no TVs, vintage radios, and iron bed frames. And, of course, there are the requisite haunted rooms that any truly historic hotel sports. But it also keeps up with the current culture with its popular restaurant—the Cup Café—its trendy Club Congress bar, and its attractive Copper Hall, scene of special events.

311 E Congress St., 520-622-8848
hotelcongress.com

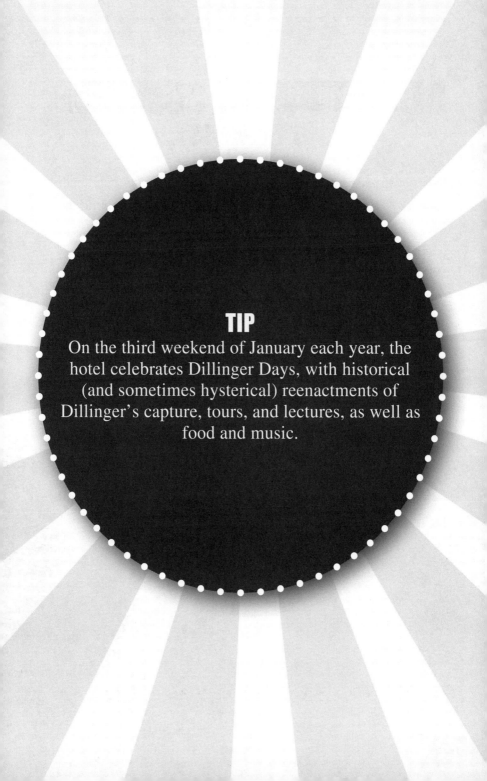

TIP

On the third weekend of January each year, the hotel celebrates Dillinger Days, with historical (and sometimes hysterical) reenactments of Dillinger's capture, tours, and lectures, as well as food and music.

RECAPTURE THE ROMANCE
OF THE RAILS

When railroads first arrived in Tucson in 1880, the then-small town proved to be a vital link in a network that helped build the West. The Historic Train Depot, which dates from 1907, was restored in 2004 and now serves as Tucson's Amtrak station. While passenger trains are less frequent these days, freight trains roll through regularly.

The depot area is rich with history. Polished wooden seating and vintage photos hark back to an earlier time. Just down the way stands the powerful 1900-era engine of Locomotive 1673, which hauled freight for the Southern Pacific for a half century and appeared in the 1955 film *Oklahoma!*.

Nearby, a statue of Wyatt Earp and Doc Holliday marks the spot of an 1882 shooting. And around the corner, the Southern Arizona Transportation Museum (414 N Toole Ave.) is crammed with colorful memorabilia and exhibits depicting local railway history.

400 N Toole Ave., 520-623-2223
tucsonhistoricdepot.org

HEAD OUT
TO A HISTORIC SPANISH MISSION

The gleaming Mission San Xavier del Bac, known as the "White Dove of the Desert," is located nine miles south of downtown Tucson on the Tohono O'odham reservation. Occupying an earlier mission site founded by a Spanish priest in 1692, the current church—built from 1783 to 1797 when the land was still part of New Spain—ranks among the premier examples of Spanish Colonial architecture in America. It's also Arizona's oldest standing European structure and a National Historic Landmark, highlighted by views of original sculptures and painted murals from the 1700s.

The mission remains an active church serving the Tohono O'odham people. A museum and video offer historical background, while a gift shop sells Tohono O'odham basketry and other native crafts.

1950 W San Xavier Rd. (exit 92 off I-19 S), 520-294-2624
sanxaviermission.org

TIP
The mission offers free admission to visitors from 7 a.m. to 5 p.m. daily, except during religious services. Check the website for mass schedules. You may also encounter disruptions due to ongoing renovation work.

ENCOUNTER ART
ON THE CUTTING EDGE

Tucson has other museums that include contemporary art among their displays, but the Museum of Contemporary Art (MOCA) is the only one to make it its entire focus. A quarter-century after it opened, MOCA remains on the cutting edge of the art world, staging an eclectic series of exhibitions that test the limits of the creative imagination—and, in some viewers' minds, what constitutes art itself.

You'll find Tucson artists represented here along with works from nationally and internationally known painters, sculptors, and other creators of the visual arts. But more importantly to a museum whose stated mission is to "inspire new ways of thinking," MOCA showcases artworks that—whether they delight or disturb our sensibilities—will challenge conventional notions about the essence of modern life and aesthetics.

265 S Church Ave., 520-624-5019
moca-tucson.org

STEP INTO
SAINT AUGUSTINE CATHEDRAL

One of downtown Tucson's most architecturally distinctive structures, the Saint Augustine Cathedral is best known for its fanciful cast-sandstone façade that depicts various desert plants and animals—saguaros, yuccas, horned toads—as well as a bronze statue of St. Augustine, the city's patron saint.

The cathedral's current design dates from 1928, when it was transformed from Romanesque Revival into Spanish Colonial Revival style, modeled after a cathedral in northern Mexico. The interior, which displays murals, mosaics, and stained-glass windows along the walls and a 12th-century crucifix behind the altar, was rebuilt in 1968, 100 years after completion of the first cathedral on the site.

The cathedral holds several Roman Catholic masses during the week. The 8 a.m. Spanish-language Sunday mass is especially noteworthy, featuring festive mariachi music.

192 S Stone Ave., 520-623-6351
cathedral-staugustine.org

TIP
Check the website for times of docent-led cathedral tours.

TRAVEL TO THE TROPICS
AT BIOSPHERE 2

Where can you go in the Tucson area to encounter a rainforest filled with tropical trees? How about a mangrove swamp, or even a million-gallon mini-ocean? All that and more can be found at Biosphere 2, a University of Arizona scientific research, training, and educational facility that replicates exotic world environments in a futuristic desert setting.

Altogether, Biosphere 2 houses seven model ecosystems—most a far cry from Tucson's own landscapes. Working with these models, scientists from several different fields carry out experiments to discover how environmental change affects various areas of the planet.

Tours take you along indoor-outdoor trails that lead to the rainforest, an ocean-viewing gallery, and other areas. The multi-shaped, mostly glass-covered facilities—which resemble something out of science fiction and were originally built as the centerpiece of a failed human endurance test—are remarkable sights in themselves.

32540 S Biosphere Rd., Oracle, 520-838-6200
biosphere2.org

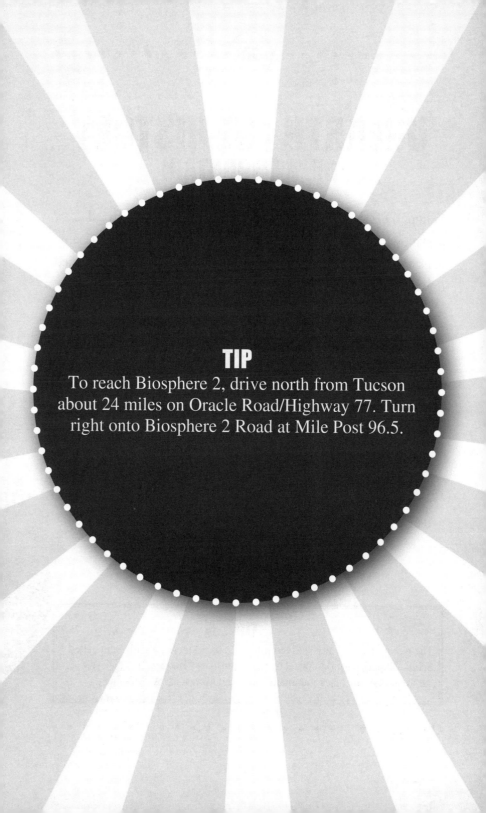

TIP

To reach Biosphere 2, drive north from Tucson about 24 miles on Oracle Road/Highway 77. Turn right onto Biosphere 2 Road at Mile Post 96.5.

UNEARTH THE HISTORY
OF "A" MOUNTAIN

Sentinel Peak, which rises 2,900 feet on the western edge of downtown across from Tumamoc Hill, acquired its official name back in pioneer days when sentinels posted atop the peak rushed down to warn of an impending Apache attack.

Tucsonans, though, know it better as "A" Mountain. One glance tells you why: the huge "A," constructed of white-painted rocks and forming the University of Arizona logo, which embellishes its eastern side. First built in 1915 to celebrate a football victory, the "A" is now repainted annually by university students.

You can drive about two-thirds of the way up Sentinel Peak, park in the lot, and walk the rocky trails that lead to the summit for wide-ranging views. You'll be treading the same hillsides inhabited by Native Americans for 4,000 years before the Spanish arrived.

1001 S Sentinel Peak Rd., 520-791-4873 (Tucson Parks and Recreation)
tucsonaz.gov/parks/sentinelpeakpark

TIP
The name "Tucson" was derived from a Native American settlement called Schuk-Shon (later pronounced by the Spanish as "Tuk-Son"), which stood "at the foot of the black mountain" now best known as "A" Mountain.

DISCOVER DESERT ART
AT TUCSON DART

Opened in 2013, the Tucson Desert Art Museum (Tucson DART) views its mission as helping visitors "visualize history through art." The history is that of the desert Southwest, and the art is a striking collection of textiles, paintings, and artifacts that are attractively displayed in spacious galleries.

Among the museum's prized items are pre-1940s Navajo and Hopi textiles, including chiefs' blankets, saddle blankets, and Yei weavings. Paintings include works by celebrated 19th- and early 20th-century landscape artists Thomas Moran and Albert Bierstadt, and more contemporary works by Peter Nisbet and Howard Post.

Mesoamerican artifacts, photos, maps, and exhibits on Navajo sand painting and early armaments help to further illuminate the cultures of the region. The museum also presents special exhibitions that change each year.

7000 E Tanque Verde Rd., 520-202-3888
tucsondart.org

GAZE AT A GALLERY
OF OPEN-AIR ART

Tucson has long been a magnet for muralists, who have transformed many city walls and buildings into an open-air gallery of big, bold, and often fanciful or amusing artworks.

Most of the artists are local, while some just temporarily dropped into town to leave their marks and move on. Some murals have been publicly funded, while others have been commissioned by businesses and nonprofit arts organizations, schools, or hospitals. But they're there for all to enjoy.

TIP

Herbert Alley off East Congress Street has changing wall murals promoting upcoming concerts at the Rialto Theatre that are up for just a few weeks or months—so take pictures.

Goddess of Agave, by Rock Martinez
440 N 7th Ave.

Bill Walton Riding a Jackalope, by Ignacio Garcia
318 E Congress St. (by the Rialto Theatre)

Greetings from Tucson, by Victor Ving
and Lisa Beggs
406 N 6th Ave. (in the alley behind Miller's Surplus)

Epic Rides (tortoise, javelina, and jackrabbit chasing
a cowboy and woman on bikes), by Joe Pagac
534 N Stone Ave. at 6th Street

World City of Gastronomy, by Ashley White
6502 E Tanque Verde Rd. (at Zio Peppe restaurant)

Mustachioed Man Skeleton, by Danny Martin
1838 E 6th St. (at Momo's)

Roadrunner, Rattlesnake and Horny Toad,
by Joe Pagac
601 N Stone Ave.

Amazing Discoveries, by Jessica Gonzales
238 S Tucson Blvd.

SOAR THROUGH THE UNIVERSE
AT UA'S PLANETARIUM

The 43,000-student University of Arizona is one of the main engines driving Tucson's cultural train. A walk around its sunny, pleasant campus will lead you to its first building—the centrally located 1891 "Old Main"—past trees and plants from arid regions around the world that form a surprisingly green urban arboretum, as well as several museums. You can even be transported into deep space.

The star of the Flandrau Science Center and Planetarium is the state-of-the-art Eco Planetarium Theater, where 360-degree dome shows whisk you from the depths of the oceans to the far corners of the universe. Most shows are geared to general audiences, though some are designed especially for kids and others for adults. (Check the website for schedules and advance tickets.) The Science Center also offers kid-friendly, hands-on astronomy, geology, and ecology exhibits.

1601 E University Blvd., 520-621-4516
flandrau.org

TIP
For more information about the UA campus and free walking tours offered during the spring and fall semesters, visit the UA Visitor Center.
811 N Euclid Ave., 520-621-5130, visitorcenter.arizona.edu

When on campus, you can also check out these first-rate museums:

Arizona State Museum: The region's oldest and largest anthropological museum displays the world's most comprehensive collection of Southwest Native American pottery and basketry.
1013 E University Blvd., 520-621-6302
statemuseum.arizona.edu

Arizona History Museum: Run by the Arizona Historical Society, this museum traces the state's history with colorful displays of artifacts and themed galleries.
949 E 2nd St., 520-628-5774
arizonahistoricalsociety.org

Museum of Art: The university's art museum showcases eight centuries of eclectic works, including paintings by Jackson Pollock and Georgia O'Keeffe.
1031 N Olive Rd., 520-621-7567
artmuseum.arizona.edu

Richard F. Caris Mirror Lab: Guided tours (Monday through Friday) introduce you to the world's largest, most advanced telescope mirrors—lightweight yet powerful—and how they're produced.
527 National Championship Dr., 520-626-8792
mirrorlab.arizona.edu

SPEND A DAY
IN TOMBSTONE AND BISBEE

Tombstone, Arizona, 70 miles southeast of Tucson, was the legendary site of the famed 1881 Gunfight at the OK Corral—where Wyatt Earp and Doc Holliday battled the Clanton Gang—and of Boothill, where cowboys were buried with their spurs on. On a day trip from Tucson, you can watch reenactments of the gunfight, visit the *Tombstone Epitaph* newspaper office, down a snifter at Big Nose Kate's Saloon, and pay your respects at Boothill. It's part history, part hokum, and on most everyone's must-do list.

Lesser-known Bisbee, Arizona, another 23 miles south of Tombstone, was once the largest town between San Francisco and St. Louis. It's a mile-high, former copper-mining center that retains its authentic Old West feel while offering up-to-date amenities and underground mine tours.

Tombstone
OK Corral: 326 E Allen St., 520-457-3456
okcorral.com

Big Nose Kate's Saloon: 417 E Allen St., 520 457-3107
bignosekatestombstone.com

Bisbee
Queen Mine Tour: 520-432-2071
queenminetour.com

Bisbee Mining & Historical Museum: 5 Copper Queen Plaza, 520-432-7071
bisbeemuseum.org

TIP

With an early start, you can visit both Tombstone and Bisbee in a day and arrive back in Tucson by sundown—or make a weekend of it.

SHOPPING AND FASHION

BROWSE FOR BARGAINS AND BLISS
ON 4TH AVENUE

North 4th Avenue between University Boulevard and 8th Street transplants a bit of San Francisco's Haight-Ashbury and New York's Greenwich Village to the city while adding some uniquely Tucson twists. It's a colorful scene blending upscale boutiques with thrift shops, burger joints with designer cafés, tattoo parlors with hair salons, food co-ops with indie bookstores (Antigone Books is the city's best) and just about anything else that falls between the hip, the trendy, and the totally off-the-wall.

It's near the University of Arizona campus, so much of its clientele is young (though the eternally youthful hang out here, too). Some of the most intriguing shops are so eclectic they're impossible to categorize—browsing works best. But you may come upon vintage clothing, bronze Buddhas, Mexican rugs, antique furniture, wacky greeting cards, classic movie posters, and much more—sometimes all in the same shop.

fourthavenue.org

TIP
Each March and December, North 4th Avenue closes to traffic as hundreds of vendors from across the country set up booths at two of Tucson's most popular street fairs. Food trucks and live entertainment add to the festivities.

MINE FOR TREASURES
AT THE GEM SHOW

Tucson's annual Gem, Mineral, and Fossil Showcase is the largest event of its kind on the planet, drawing tens of thousands of bling lovers, rockhounds, and fossil fans for a two-week extravaganza each winter.

Housed in some 50 mostly downtown venues ranging from hotels to giant tents, the showcase attracts hundreds of global dealers offering eye-popping displays. Whether you're after a $2 polished agate, a $200,000 necklace, an onyx lamp, or a fossilized dinosaur skeleton, you can find it here. Most shows run from late January to mid-February, just in time to purchase a bauble for Valentine's Day.

It all began modestly in 1955 with the original Gem & Mineral Show, which, over time, spawned the many satellite shows. The original remains the marquee event, filling the Convention Center for four days in mid-February.

Gem, Mineral, and Fossil Showcase
tucsongemshows.net

Gem & Mineral Show
Tucson Convention Center, 260 S Church Ave.
tgms.org/show

TIP
Dealers often offer big discounts toward the end of the shows.

DRESS LIKE A WILDCAT
IN UA GEAR

One sure sign that you attended the University of Arizona, or wished you'd gone to UA . . . or you watch UA games on TV . . . or you live in or near Tucson . . . or you recently arrived and just want to fit in, is that you're wearing some type of Arizona Wildcat gear.

It could be a red or blue T-shirt or sweatshirt emblazoned with the "A" logo, the snarling face of a wildcat, or simply "Arizona." It could be a baseball cap, basketball jersey, gym shorts, or colorful socks. None of that really matters. The crucial thing is that as soon as you don the gear, you won't be mistaken for a fan of the arch-rival Arizona State Sun Devils. Go Cats!

You can buy official Wildcat gear at the Student Union Memorial Center or at any UA BookStore or A-Store branch.

1209 E University Blvd., 520-621-2426
shop.arizona.edu

TIP

Most Wildcat merchandise is 25 percent off at UA BookStores during "Bear Down Sales" the day before home football games. You can also shop thriftily online those days at shop.arizona.edu (using promo code "beardown").

PICK UP NATIVE PLANTS
AT DESERT SURVIVORS

The Tucson area has a number of cactus nurseries, but the nonprofit Desert Survivors, which nurtures some 600 plant species native to the Sonoran Desert, has some special qualities. For starters, it's a short drive from downtown, with easy access from north or south just west of Interstate 10. The docents there are extremely knowledgeable and can advise you on which plants thrive best in sunshine or in shadow. And all the plants for sale have been cultivated by adults with developmental disabilities, providing much-needed jobs.

For creating your own desert landscape at home, you'll find many species of cacti—including barrels, prickly pears, chollas, and saguaros—as well as agaves, grasses, and young palo verde trees. Many plants are conveniently sold in one- or two-gallon pots that can later be transplanted if you wish.

1020 Starr Pass Blvd., 520-791-9309
desertsurvivors.org

TIP
Ask about the availability of special Mission Heritage Fruit Trees, which were first introduced by Spanish missionaries in the late 1600s and include figs, pomegranates, and quince.

WANDER THROUGH THE MAZE
AT OLD TOWN ARTISANS

Care for a sprinkling of history with your shopping experience? At Old Town Artisans, which fills an entire block in the Presidio district (Tucson's oldest neighborhood), you can wander through a half-dozen shops and galleries occupying adobes dating from the 1850s. These are Arizona's longest continuously occupied buildings, with ceilings fashioned from improvised materials: saguaro cactus ribs, packing crates, and whiskey barrel staves.

One shop feeds into the next in a kind of rabbit-warren layout, leading you through a maze of products and merchandise: custom jewelry, fine art, vintage clothing, mesquite lamps, Native American pottery, vinyl records, artisan pasta and bread, and quirky gift items galore. You can even get yourself a tattoo if you'd like, "at a place your Mom would want you to get a tattoo." (Well, maybe.)

201 N Court Ave., with entrances on Court and Meyer avenues
and Washington and Telles streets, 520-622-0351
oldtownartisans.com

TIP
After shopping, take a breather in the complex's shady inner courtyard, where there's an excellent restaurant, a pub, and often live music.

TREK ON UP
TO THE NATIONAL PARKS STORE

Even the folks who run Tucson's National Parks Store admit it's off the beaten path, but they insist "It's worth the trip!" And they're right. Once you're there, off the highway and miles north of the central city, you'll be rewarded by one of the region's best selections of authentic Native American art, jewelry, and textiles, as well as handmade Mexican crafts. The pottery from Mata Ortiz (a Mexican artists' village) and woven Tarahumara baskets are worth the trip by themselves.

Add to this a superior selection of regional travel and nature books, including a large kids' section focusing on local wildlife, as well as a plethora of park guides, cards, stuffed animals, puzzles, and toys (purchases are tax free and help support national parks). The store also holds regular events ranging from book talks to lectures on nature and indigenous arts and crafts.

12880 N Vistoso Village Dr., Oro Valley, 520-622-1999
wnpa.org/national-parks-store

TIP
The store is located near the foothills of the Santa Catalina Mountains, which may inspire you to do some hiking at nearby Catalina State Park—scenic enough to be a national park itself.

BRIGHTEN YOUR OUTDOOR DECOR
AT LOYA'S

You get a two-fer here. Entering through the gates of Mexican Garden Pottery, one of Tucson's largest purveyors of Mexican garden pots and planters, you'll find a great variety in sizes and styles, including brightly colored, hand-painted Talavera pots. It's a longstanding family-owned business run by the family matriarch.

More recently, son Danny opened Loya's Courtyard adjacent to Mexican Garden Pottery (just keep walking), and he has outdone his mom in terms of sheer spectacle. You can find almost anything you want for your outdoor decor here, from ceramic pots to stone fountains and wrought-iron tables topped with colorful Mexican tiles—or even strikingly huge metal sculptures of dinosaurs and other beasts. Danny designs and commissions them from Mexican artists, and they're guaranteed to make your outdoor garden stand out, in a *Jurassic Park* sort of way. Even if you don't buy one, they're sure to brighten your shopping experience.

Loya's Courtyard
2925 N Oracle Rd., 520-882-8892
loyascourtyard.com

Mexican Garden Pottery
2901 N Oracle Rd., 520-624-4772

DELVE INTO FINE ART
AT DESERT ARTISANS

A consortium of regional artists and artisans own and operate this jewel of a gallery tucked away in a small shopping mall on Tucson's east side. For more than 30 years, the artisans have banded together to cooperatively display and sell their work: exquisite jewelry, stunning glassware, colorful paintings and photographs, and beautifully crafted ceramics and basketry. More than 60 local artists contribute, many with their own labeled space in the gallery.

Notable works include clay sculptures of Native Americans by Terry Slonaker, sparkling glass jewelry by Margaret Shirer, and paintings of desert blossoms by Jan Thompson. When you visit the Desert Artisans Gallery, you're likely to meet one of the artists at the front counter; they take turns handling sales duties.

6536 E Tanque Verde Rd. (in the La Plaza Shoppes mall), 520-722-4412
desertartisansgallery.com

TIP
The La Plaza Shoppes mall contains a few other
small art galleries as well, which you may want to browse.

UNLOCK THE SECRETS
OF THE WAREHOUSE ARTS DISTRICT

Tucson's Warehouse Arts District emerged during the 1980s when the state of Arizona bought up blocks of neglected warehouses downtown to make way for a highway. When that plan fell through, the state rented the spaces to artists at low cost, and artists have remained and thrived there ever since, helping to revitalize downtown in the process.

Along East Toole Avenue and elsewhere in the district, you'll find shared artists' studio spaces, fashion designers, photographers, performance artists, and more. The 1907-era Steinfeld Warehouse (101 West 6th Street, 520-237-1875) is one prominent studio and exhibition space for artists.

Not all the arts spaces have galleries or retail outlets, so you may encounter lots of closed doors. But a stroll around the area can yield some off-the-beaten-track gems, such as the Santa Theresa Tile Works (440 North 6th Avenue, 520-623-8640), where you can design your own mini-masterpieces made with fanciful tiles.

wamotucson.org

TIP
The Warehouse Arts District is bounded roughly by East Toole Avenue and West 6th Street west of the railroad tracks and by East 5th Street, North 4th Avenue, and East 8th Street to the north and east of the tracks.

TOP OFF YOUR DUDS
AT ARIZONA HATTERS

At some point in Tucson—maybe attending the rodeo, dancing at a country-western bar, staying at a dude ranch, or just trying to keep the sun from burning your head—you may hanker for a real cowboy hat (also known as a Western hat). If so, look no further than Arizona Hatters, where you'll find a wide selection of sizes, styles, colors, and brands including Stetson, Bailey, and Atwood. Arizona Hatters offers custom fits for men, women, and children, with hand-sewn sweat bands and liners, brim cutting, padding, and stretching. They'll also repair or reshape your old hat.

To help complete the urban cowboy look, you can select a hatband (including hand-made beaded ones), as well as accessories like silk scarves, bolo ties, shirts, vests, and belts. Just add boots and a horse and you're ready to gallop off into the Tucson Mountains sunset.

2790 N Campbell Ave., 520-292-1320
arizonahatters.com

TIP
Not into the cowboy look? Arizona Hatters carries an impressive array of other types of hats to suit or reshape your personality, ranging from Panama to pork pie, fedora to bowler, cap to top hat, and more.

FIND YOUR FANCY
AT THE LOST BARRIO SHOPS

Tucson's Lost Barrio isn't actually lost—it's not even missing. And that's all to the good, because a three-block-long row of some of the city's most intriguing shops awaits you there in plain sight.

The neighborhood, a historic warehouse district more formally known as Barrio San Antonio, acquired its "Lost" moniker when past highway construction severed it from some adjoining neighborhoods.

You can browse the shops for handcrafted imports, custom furniture, antiques, folk art, fine art, lighting accessories, and more from Tucson and around the globe.

TIP
Access South Park Avenue from
East Broadway Boulevard near Euclid Avenue, just east of downtown.

Colonial Frontiers: Antiques, folk art
244 S Park Ave., 520-622-7400
colonialfrontiers.com

Felix: Handcrafted wooden,
wrought-iron, and copper furniture
228 S Park Ave., 520-833-1794
felixtucson.com

La Casa Mexicana: Mexican furniture
204 S Park Ave., 520-624-1420
lcm-interiors.com

Lost Barrio Gallery: Hand-crafted
furniture and restoration
208 S Park Ave., 520-623-9856
lostbarriogallery.com

Rustica: Mexican and Peruvian
furniture and folk art
200 S Park Ave., 520-623-4435
rusticatucson.com

Southwest Furniture & Design: Handcrafted
furniture from the same owners as Felix
212 S Park Ave., 520-461-1341
azsouthwestfurniture.com

HOP ABOARD SUN LINK
FOR DOWNTOWN SHOPPING

The verdict is in: Tucson's 2014-built Sun Link streetcar system has played a key role in revitalizing downtown and spurring the growth of shops, restaurants, bars, theaters, residential buildings, and varied businesses along its entire route. The streetcars wind from the University of Arizona area (home to the North 4th Avenue shopping district, Main Gate Square, university bookstores, and other heavily patronized shops) to the Mercado San Agustin public marketplace just west of downtown.

Along the nearly four-mile route, Sun Link cuts through the heart of the city while making a total of 23 stops that connect to some 150 shops within easy walking distance. The streetcars run from 7 a.m. to 10 p.m. Monday through Wednesday, 7 a.m. to 2 a.m. Thursday and Friday, 8 a.m. to 2 a.m. Saturday, and 8 a.m. to 8 p.m. Sunday. Late-night hours are shorter Thursday through Saturday when UA is on summer or winter break.

520-792-9222
suntran.com

TIP

Buy SunGO transit tickets or passes at any streetcar stop, or download them to your smartphone using the Go Tucson Transit mobile app. You cannot pay once on board.

GO RETRO
AT TOM'S FINE FURNITURE

"When New Isn't Good Enough" is the slogan at Tom's Fine Furniture and Collectables, and when you enter one of his three stores you may well start thinking retro for your home decor.

Since 1981, Tom Ward has probably sold more second-hand sofas, lamps, mirrors, rugs, artworks, silverware and china sets, antiques, and vintage clothing and jewelry to Tucson residents than anyone else. And he celebrates the "used" part, contending that the "furniture our parents and grandparents owned was crafted from better materials and was made to last for generations." Real wood! Screws or pegs instead of staples! Eight-way hand-tied springs! Try to find that at IKEA.

Tom's 10,000-square-foot "super store" on Pima Street contains the widest selection of items, while the other two stores add outdoor furniture and more vintage items to the mix.

5454 E Pima St., 520-795-5210
4101 E Grant Rd., 520-777-8188
3402 E Grant Rd., 520-321-4621
tomsfurnituretucson.com

TIP
You can also sell things to Tom, but they must
be of suitable quality, condition, and desirability to customers.

SPARK UP YOUR DAY
AT SONORAN GLASS

You have two options for finding your fire at the Sonoran Glass School, southern Arizona's top center for all things glass. One is to browse the gallery and sculpture garden to shop for glass-art gifts, decorative pieces, and glassware made by school faculty, students, and visiting artists. (Sales benefit the nonprofit school.)

The other is to join a class to try your hand (and lung power) at fashioning your own glass creations, choosing your own colors and designs for vases and bowls, in the glassblowing studio. Other classes are offered in torchworking for making glass sculptures and kiln-fusing for working with sheet glass. You can even test your mettle at a "Make Your Own Experiences" one-day class (a nice option for visitors); individuals, couples, and families can participate. If you wish, you can just observe a class, or, if you're with a group, ask about arranging a guided tour.

633 W 18th St., 520-884-7814
sonoranglass.org

TIP
For any activity, call ahead for the schedule
on the day you'd like to visit and to make an appointment.

SHOP FARMERS' MARKETS
FOR FRESH FOODS

The Tucson food scene is trending heavily toward fresh foods and local sourcing from organic farms, along with locally crafted specialty items. That should point you straight in the direction of the city's growing array of farmers' markets, which operate year-round (though at different days of the week and times of day).

Community Food Bank of Southern Arizona
3003 S Country Club Rd., 520-882-3304, Tuesdays 8 a.m. to noon

Heirloom Farmers' Market
Rillito Park, 4502 N 1st Ave., 520-882-2157, Sundays 9 a.m. to 1 p.m.
October to mid-April, 8 a.m. to noon mid-April to September

Heirloom Farmers' Market East
Morris K. Udall Park, 7202 E Tanque Verde Rd., 520-882-2157, Fridays 9 a.m.
to 1 p.m. October to mid-April; 8 a.m. to noon mid-April to September

Heirloom Farmers' Market Oro Valley
Steam Pump Ranch, 10901 N Oracle Rd., Oro Valley, 520-882-2157, Saturdays
9 a.m. to 1 p.m. October to mid-April, 8 a.m. to noon mid-April to September

Heirloom Rincon Valley Farmers' and Artisans' Market
12500 E Old Spanish Trail, 520-882-2157, Saturdays 9 a.m. to 1 p.m. October
to mid-April; 8 a.m. to noon mid-April to September

Santa Cruz River Farmers' Market
Mercado San Agustin, 100 S Avenida del Convento, 520-882-3304, Thursdays
4 p.m. to 7 p.m. May to September; 3 p.m. to 6 p.m. October to April

COUNT ON HIGH QUALITY
AT MUSEUM SHOPS

Some of the most interesting shopping in town can be found within Tucson's museums and botanical gardens.

While specific items and emphases vary from shop to shop, these are reliable places to browse for high-quality, authentic jewelry, basketry, pottery, textiles, glasswork, carvings, and crafts—often the works of local and Southwestern artisans as well as those of Native Americans from several tribal nations.

You'll also find eclectic selections of regional books and products as well as children's sections featuring books, toys, and puzzles.

Arizona State Museum
1013 E University Blvd.
520-626-5886
statemuseum.arizona.edu

Tucson Desert Art Museum
7000 E Tanque Verde Rd.
520-202-3888
tucsondart.org

Tohono Chul
7366 N Paseo Del Norte
520-742-6455
tohonochulpark.org

Tucson Museum of Art
140 N Main Ave.
520-624-2333
tucsonmuseumofart.org

Tucson Botanical Gardens
2150 N Alvernon Way
520-326-9686
tucsonbotanical.org

PAY A MOONLIT VISIT
TO METAL ARTS VILLAGE

Housing independent artists and artisans working in a variety of genres (primarily metal sculpture, but you might also find painting, custom-designed stained-glass, photography, or even award-winning tattoo artists), Metal Arts Village is the creation of attorney-sculptor Stephen Kimble, who designed and built the attractive complex in 2009. The Village is now under new management, and several of the artist-tenants are changing.

Since these are working studios, not retail operations, buying opportunities from most of the artists are limited to "chance or by appointment." You might catch one or more on site, but a prior appointment is much safer. Watch for periodic open houses that incorporate the award-winning Tucson Hop Shop (520-908-7765), where local craft beers star in an urban beer garden. An expanded music stage has been moved nearer to the Hop Shop for live performances.

3230 N Dodge Blvd., 520-529-1300

TIP
One of the studios is occupied by Beads of Courage, a nonprofit that donates hand-made beads to children with serious illnesses. Each bead commemorates a milestone they have conquered during treatments, helping provide the courage to continue.
520-344-7668, beadsofcourage.org

ENJOY RELAXED SHOPPING
AT LA ENCANTADA

La Encantada is the most pleasant shopping mall in Tucson. Set in the foothills of the Catalina Mountains overlooking the city, it's an upscale, Spanish-style complex that's user-friendly from start to finish.

First, head for the covered parking—a big plus on scorching hot days—and continue a short distance to the open-air, bi-level mall, which is pedestrian-only with shaded walkways. The boutique-sized shops are primarily mid- to upper-level chains, featuring clothing, jewelry, cosmetics, furniture, and housewares. But you'll also find top-quality regional outlets such as Savaya Coffee Market, AJ's Fine Foods, and the Southern Arizona Arts Guild Gallery.

The lower-level courtyard is replete with orange trees, bougainvillea, fountains, and patio tables with chairs. Several good restaurants and lounges offer both indoor and outdoor seating.

2905 E Skyline Dr. at N Campbell Ave., 520-276-3800
laencantadashoppingcenter.com

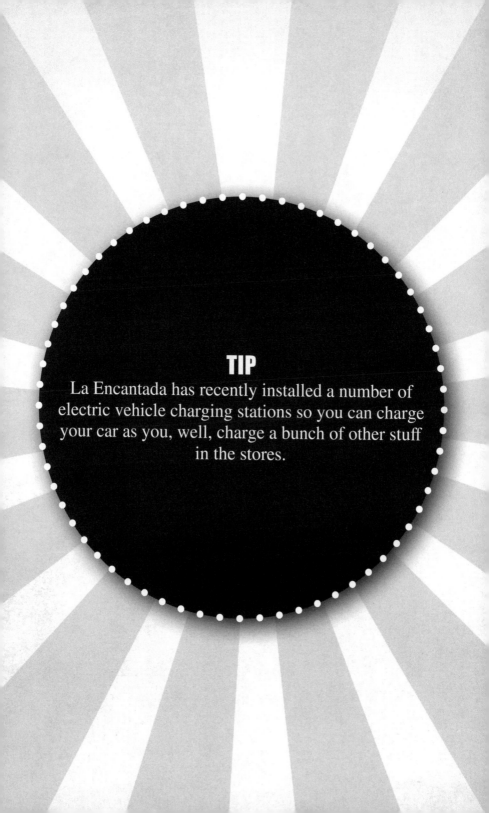

TIP

La Encantada has recently installed a number of electric vehicle charging stations so you can charge your car as you, well, charge a bunch of other stuff in the stores.

SUGGESTED
ITINERARIES

KID FRIENDLY

ONLY IN TUCSON

SPECIAL OCCASION

ROUGH & READY

FREE ACTIVITIES

OFF THE BEATEN PATH

ACTIVITIES
BY SEASON

Much of Tucson takes the summer off—or takes off for the summer—because of the typically intense heat. Be advised that strenuous outdoor activity such as hiking can be dangerous in summer. (Carry lots of water, wear sun protection, and let someone know your plans.) In general, winter is Tucson's busiest season, but many activities take place from October to April, and most attractions stay open year-round, sometimes with shorter hours.

WINTER

SPRING

SUMMER

FALL

INDEX